THE ORDEAL

A Journey from Misfortunes, Illness, and Betrayal to Truth

Josephine Walden

Copyright © 2022 Josephine Walden

All rights reserved

The characters and events portrayed in this book are fictitious. Any similarity to real persons, living or dead, is coincidental and not intended by the author.

No part of this book may be reproduced, or stored in a retrieval system, or transmitted in any form or by any means, electronic, mechanical, photocopying, recording, or otherwise, without express written permission of the publisher.

ISBN-13: 979-8847402897

Printed in the United States of America

"I would be true, for there are those who trust me;

I would be pure, for there are those who care;

I would be strong, for there is much to suffer;

I would be brave, for there is much to dare."

My Creed

By

Howard Arnold Walter

CONTENTS

Title Page
Copyright
Epigraph
Preface

One	1
Two	13
Three	28
Four	34
Five	45
Six	65
Seven	87
Eight	100
Nine	108
Ten	121
Eleven	145
Twelve	167
Thirteen	194
Fourteen	205

Fifteen	246
Sixteen	270
Seventeen	288
Eighteen	298
Nineteen	311
Twenty	331
Twenty-One	361
Epilogue	389
Acknowledgement	393
About The Author	395

PREFACE

We never know what we are destined to experience in our lifetimes. For some, life seems to run a smooth course, filled with some positive and fulfilling experiences. For others, life may present a more difficult path.

Growing up in a small town on the Great Lakes was, in my mind, special. Everyone knew everyone, some of the families had lived in the area for many years. We knew who the nice people were and the not so nice.

As my sister and I played in the neighborhood, we could stop in at either grandparents' and have a peanut butter sandwich under a shade tree or lemonade and cookies— with a side of warm welcomes and big hugs. We were free to ride our bikes everywhere and go swimming. It was a peaceful, laid-back life and a great place to grow up.

As my sister and I grew into teenagers, Mom tried to teach us to be as prepared as one could for life's precipitous declines such as economic downturns and natural disasters, even though we had never experienced floods and tornadoes. Weather around the lakes was stable. Aunt

Beckie was often presented as an example of why one should be prepared for the downturns in life. She had her degree in Art and Music and minored in Elementary Education. A few years into her marriage, her husband became ill with a chronic condition that required intermittent, long hospitalization. He would never be able to work again. Their only child, a son, died from the same disease her husband suffered. Devastated, she somehow worked her way through a depression and for the rest of her life taught school and drove long miles to visit Uncle Ernie, her husband, without complaint. Her teaching was creative yet thorough. Her extraordinary efforts were recognized by the school administrators. The kids who had never done very well in school produced for her. The students and their parents loved her. She had an inspiring, positive attitude and a deep faith. She had given her whole heart and soul to her teaching—and to my sister and me. The question Mom always presented to us was, "Where would she have been without the broad education she had gotten?" The question most on my mind was, "Where would she have been without that indomitable spirit?" I was convinced one needed both.

Despite having a deep love for music and being very musical, I didn't want to teach music. I made plans to attend college and major in Business, but I eventually switched to nursing school. I married and had a child, but after seventeen years my husband and I divorced.

During my years of working, I budgeted and saved in case of any of those unforeseen problems I had been warned about growing up. My feeling was that, despite making mistakes in my life, I was now on solid ground. Nursing had been a great choice, not only because it was fulfilling to be able to help others but because what one learned could be used for an entire lifetime. I felt optimistic about my future. Life was good!

With all that said, no matter how prepared I thought I was for any untoward events that might come my way, disasters occurred that decimated my savings. Then, the unthinkable happened. A little understood and devastating illness struck. My life was irreparably changed. Added to that was the loss of my family and then betrayal by someone I implicitly trusted.

Every ethical and moral part of my being was challenged. Could I muster the strength I needed to fight this? My thoughts turned to Aunt Beckie and the strength she had shown during her long crisis. Important elements were at stake here: truth and integrity. I decided to pursue the truth. Later, my health improved somewhat and, when I distanced myself from certain stressful triggers, the total picture became clear, though there was still a great deal of emotional pain. Bothered by these events, and with my background as a former nurse-counselor, I knew it would be therapeutic to write about it. It helped me to better understand and deal with that traumatic time, giving me more insight. My stress was relieved, and my goal accomplished.

Years later, in sorting through junk in our attic, I unearthed the papers relevant to those past events, some of which were typed at the time in an attempt to vent and record what had happened. My thought at the time was that, in looking back, the events wouldn't seem as traumatic. However, the more I read, the more appalled I became.

Reviewing all the material, a realization hit me. The deceptive and negative behavior I endured was not only wide ranging, it was carefully planned.

The decision to write this book evolved from that time on. The unpredictability of human behavior had always fascinated me, and I thought this unusual time in my life might make for an interesting read. There are questions even today to which I will never know the answers. I have included a fair amount of childhood history, which I felt was necessary to understand certain future events.

The names and places in this true story have been changed for the sake of anonymity. The material was taken from my original "therapeutic" attempt to analyze what had happened, as well as from a diary with descriptions of the day-to-day struggles with traumatic occurrences in my life and the symptoms of a little understood illness. Also included are the typewritten accounts of dialogue and behavior recorded at the time of the incidents, as well as letters, court records, attorneys' comments, and witness observations.

ONE

THE JOURNEY BEGINS

1983

It all began on one of my trips to see my parents in April of 1983. I was extremely late getting home from work, had packing to do and annoyed with myself for not packing the night before, quickly fixed myself a snack, took a phone call from a friend, then was finally on my way.

The city was left behind by 7:00 pm. That meant my arrival in Williamsport would be around 11:00 pm. By this time the expressway was free of rush hour traffic and most of the trip was uneventful. About an hour out from Williamsport, I came off the expressway on to a highway. I had just left a mid-sized city with the diminution of traffic when I noticed a car steadily following me for 15 miles. We were out in the country and by this time of night the country was usually quiet and dark with only a few cars on the road.

Hoping I was worried about nothing, I slowed down in the belief that if he wanted to pass me, perhaps he would do so if my speed was slower. To my alarm, the car also slowed and continued behind me. I increased my speed but so did he! Then the car pulled up alongside of me and I could see a black seven-year-old Chevy with two men inside. They came across the line and began hitting my car on the driver's side. As we sped along, they hit me several more times. Their car was larger than mine and I struggled to hold the road. As I fought to stay on the pavement, the banging on the side of my car became more frequent and severe. Slowly I was being forced off the pavement on to the gravel shoulder! A ditch ran along each side of the road which made me wonder how to avoid that if I was forced past the shoulder.

My heart pounding, desperately I began looking for any house along this deserted stretch of road that may have had a light on. Finally at the point of no longer being able to hold the road and halfway on the shoulder, down a hill and through a large and thick number of evergreens, I thought I saw a dim light in a window. It appeared to be downhill from the highway. *Was I right*? If I was, what a miracle! I desperately hung on and sped up precipitously fast and turned in to the driveway at a reckless speed. Stopping the car just short of the house, I looked back to observe the car doing a U-turn and heading back to the city. Shaking, I knew I had to collect myself. Who lived in this small house surrounded by thick evergreens, no garage and no visible barns or outbuildings? *Was anyone there*? Overwhelming gratitude and a feeling of humility coursed through my body for whoever left that light on in the small, inconsequential home. Whoever it was or whatever it was I felt eternally blessed. All I could do was utter a prayer of thanks with the feeling that there had been a guardian angel watching over me. After taking the time to calm down and collect myself I turned the car around with the car lights falling fully on the small house. Still, no one responded, no one emerged from the house, there was no porch light, no one at the window. Finally feeling more calm, I faced the car out of the driveway. I cautiously re-entered the highway. The rest of the trip was uneventful. On my arrival I did not relate the incident to my family. I never travelled alone at night again. Little did I surmise this was just the beginning of a long and difficult ordeal.

1984

The November day of the funeral dawned gray and cool. We stood in the cemetery as frigid gusts of northerly winds blew across the region of Michigan known as "the Thumb." Fine drops of rain peppered our tear-stained faces. I, my family, and other friends and loved ones were there to say goodbye to my mother, Abigail, whose death had been unexpected. As I watched my mother's body be committed to the earth, I shifted my posture as sharp, shooting pains radiated down my right leg, symptoms I was sure were from a car accident nine months back.

The funeral had been held in a small, Victorian church, one of only twenty other buildings in the community. My family had been affiliated with the old church for years. My mother and my Aunt Beckie, along with two others, had donated their time as church organists, rotating and taking one Sunday a month.

When the services concluded, we all adjourned to the church's recently constructed addition, a spacious hall with a kitchen and great room for various events such as rummage sales, showers, and of course funerals. As we sat in folding chairs at long tables, eating home-cooked food prepared by church patrons, we reminisced and visited with other mourners and family members. My now widowed father, 86-year-old Lee, a retired teacher, was bearing up well. My sister Julie and I sat with him, along with my twenty-one-year-old daughter, Victoria, united in our grief.

My ex-husband Brad was in attendance as well. A tall, handsome man and a member of law enforcement, he had maintained a close relationship with my family even after our divorce. At one point, my father asked him if he would be kind enough to take all the funeral flowers to my parents' home. Afterward, we would distribute them to the local hospital and to shut-ins. Brad agreed, loaded up the flowers, and headed for the house.

Our home was a rambling Edwardian with six bedrooms, built in the early 1900s. It was located on probably the most scenic lot in town. When Brad arrived I was informed my two nieces, Alison and Liz, had tailed him. They offered him no assistance but followed him throughout the house as he situated the flowers, keeping him under surveillance. My ex-husband was the epitome of ethics and integrity. When Brad told me about it later, I was puzzled but made no mention of it to my father.

When the rest of the family, myself included, returned to the house, my sister and her husband Jim, Liz and her husband, my other niece and my father all sat around the kitchen table while I made cocoa for those who wanted some. Dad, Julie, and Jim elected to have a cocktail. Soon, everyone drifted off to bed and Julie and I were alone.

She looked at me, waving her second drink in the air. "You left me alone with Mother, you know," she said, her tone full of accusation, "and you should have been there!"

Startled, I answered, "Dad was with you, wasn't he?"

"No! He was exhausted and had gone home. Jim had to stay with me. It was your place to be there, not his!"

"But Julie, I needed to get back to work. There were two days left of vacation and I just didn't have the money to simply miss work until this was all resolved. The doctor didn't seem to think she would go that fast. Mother seemed relieved when I told her I had to go back to work. She welcomed one less person around." My sister didn't seem to realize what working a full-time job with three extra shifts each week meant, that bills for myself, and my daughter Victoria simply had to be paid.

Julie's voice rose and tears came to

her eyes, "She had an oxygen mask. I stayed by her bedside and tried to keep it on. She kept fighting me. When she seemed quieter, Jim and I took a break and went for coffee. While we were at the coffee shop, we were paged. When I arrived back at her room, she had taken the mask off. She was dead. Someone should have been with her! I wasn't there!"

"Julie," I said, trying to calm her, "don't blame yourself. Don't you see? Mother couldn't leave us while we were around. She knew how desperately we wanted her to live. By leaving and going on your break, it gave her that chance to bow out the way she wished. Think of it this way, she's probably ecstatic to be out of that poor, painful body! Recently, I heard about a case where the doctor was aware of that kind of situation and advised the family to leave the dying patient in peace and solitude. Some people can't do their dying with their family around. Quit blaming yourself for not being there. We all did the best we could, and Mother knows that. Mother did her dying when no one was there, and I am sure that is exactly the way she wanted it."

Julie remained silent, the recriminations gone, while I said a prayer of thanks, relieved I had been able to allay my sister's anxiety.

My job as a nurse and psychiatric nurse-counselor only allowed me five days for bereavement. During that time, the family shared their grief, wrote thank-you notes to those who had sent flowers and other sentiments, and made sure my father got settled in. We planned that he would spend the coming holidays with Julie and Jim in their beautiful home. Jim was the manager of a large sales company and Julie, a raven-haired beauty, had been a part-time nurse but had recently quit her job. I looked forward to the family spending Christmas with them, attending Christmas Eve service together, and celebrating in lovely, festive surroundings.

The five days sped by, and it was time to say goodbye. My mother's only sister and my favorite aunt, Beckie, whispered in my ear that she would love to come and live with me in my home in Illinois. My daughter and I, along with Brad, took our leave. Then Brad followed us to see us home safely.

The first Christmas without my mother was sad and difficult. Our family gathered at Julie and Jim's. On Christmas Eve, Jim helped his neighbors set out Venetian lights along their street. Many neighborhoods did the same. It made the ride to church beautiful and special. After the service, we returned home for dinner and the opening of gifts. Christmas wasn't the same without Abigail and it never would be again. The children sparkled with enthusiasm, but Dad, Julie, and I were subdued, making a supreme effort to be festive. Victoria and I left for home on Christmas Day, as I had to be at work by 3:00pm. The four-hour drive would get me back just in time to unload the car and get to work.

* * * * *

Dad ended up staying at Julie's through the winter and I called him as often as possible. When spring arrived, Julie called to report that he still didn't want to go home. She asked me what she should do. His friends were all back in the hometown, and he had plenty there to keep him busy and his adjustment could begin.

"Tell him to at least give it a try and see how he gets along," I advised her. Julie phoned me later to say that Dad agreed to give it a try.

We went to my father's home that summer over the Fourth of July, and the whole family had a few, wonderful days with parades, fireworks, and a flea market. Cousins arrived and joined in the family fun. Dad tried to enjoy the festivities, but I could see it wasn't heartfelt.

* * * * *

Three months later, Brad called. He was in the hometown on vacation and had stopped to see Dad. He sounded upset. "He can't stay alone. He's not eating well, he doesn't seem to want to see friends, and from what I can find out, people invite him to do a lot of things, but he always declines. He's throwing his Meals-on-Wheels in the freezer and drinking. If he is left here like this, he will be dead in another three months. He looks terrible." Then he added, "Don't you girls ever check on him to see how he is doing?"

"I didn't know."

"Julie's been there," he exclaimed as though unable to comprehend such a breach. "Hasn't she noticed?"

"I don't know what Julie notices or thinks about when she is there. She has not said anything. Do you want to bring him back with you and drop him at my place? I'd love to have him."

Brad said no because he felt it was a matter for my sister and me to handle. Dad had never acted this way before. I had hoped it would pass with adjustment to Mom's death. After we hung up, I called

Julie immediately. She drove the four hours to our father's house and took Dad home with her once again.

Several days later, I received an angry phone call from my sister. "I don't intend to take care of Dad alone!" she said. "If you want your inheritance, you'd just better help!"

I was struck by her anger more than her words. I had never witnessed her in such a state. "Julie, don't be upset. Of course, I will help with Dad any way I can. I will take him right now if you wish. I had to call you because Brad refused to bring him back here."

"No," she countered, appearing to relax a bit. "I will keep him six months of the year and you keep him the other six."

"Are you sure? I would be happy to take him. After all, he was with you last winter after Mother died."

Julie began to sound more like herself. "No, I would rather keep him in the winter because we spend less time at his house in the winter and it will be less stressful for him to be there less in the summer." Jim still visited his mother, who lived in the same area, monthly, and of course, there was Aunt Beckie to visit. She continued, "You keep Dad for six months over the summer because we use the house a lot then and I know he will not want to be there. Just bring him to the hometown over the Fourth of July. He should enjoy all the people who will be around."

TWO

LOVE, LOSS AND MISFORTUNE

1986 - 1987

That spring after my father arrived, Aunt Beckie's earlier request occurred to me. Dad and Aunt Beckie might enjoy each other's company. Aunt Beckie had severe arthritis and needed a walker. She couldn't climb stairs and my full bathroom was upstairs, but there was a half bath on the first floor. She could use that and with my help could be bathed daily. I could put a bed in my dining room.

Beckie was a love and they had all been so close. Strangely, when I suggested the idea to my father, he steadfastly refused the proposed plan. "If she comes here, I leave!" I was puzzled by his attitude. According to my aunt, his withdrawal and distancing from her after Mom's death had been very hurtful. No one understood what his reasons were, and he refused to give any. My assumption was that Dad was angry he had lost Mom and the closeness they had all enjoyed was too painful. Perhaps he resented that Aunt Beckie was seven years older than Mom and yet alive and well.

Dad was slowly deteriorating. He'd had a small stroke some years before and, while Mom was alive, there seemed to be negligible symptoms but now he walked with a slightly unsteady gait. His sight in one eye was gone and he feared surgery, so he lived with it. Also, he was smoking again, which did nothing for his emphysema. Despite his physical limitations, he was no trouble and I loved having him with me.

I had agonized over Dad being alone so much and tried to make it up to him. We played dominoes, went for ice cream, and sometimes he took me out to dinner. I even coaxed him into taking short walks with me. Because he was alone so much due to my extra workload, I stopped working extra shifts. It made my financial struggle more difficult. In tears, I finally called Julie, who had been handling the money since our mother's death and asked for help from Dad's expense account. Julie complied without comment.

My father's care included keeping his hair, fingernails, and toenails trimmed and making sure he bathed regularly. He didn't like showers. Dad had unruly, stubborn, black hair sprinkled with gray that had to be oiled into place every time it was cut. I called Julie to ask about how often to do these things. Julie replied off-handedly that she didn't know because she made Jim do it. I was surprised to say the least: Jim worked long hours while Julie no longer worked her two-day-a-week job. She belonged to a bridge club, played golf or bowled depending on the season, was in the church choir and lunched weekly with friends.

Dad and I did not go to the family home on the lake for the Fourth of July as Julie suggested. He was afraid of the memories it would trigger, so we stayed away.

Julie phoned at the end of August and told me to bring Dad back to Williamsport as my six months were up. She and Jim were going on a trip for three weeks and then she was going with Jim out of town on business. I expressed concern that Dad would be alone, but Julie assured me Alison and Liz stopped in often and spent time with him. Reluctantly, I packed the car and took my dad to Williamsport.

*　　*　　*　　*　　*

Approximately three weeks after I took Dad to my sister's, in August of

1986, the small, sleepy stream near my home suddenly developed into an angry, raging torrent. The water came through the storm sewer and the basement flooded half-way up the walls. All the furniture was ruined, and the furnace and dryer would no longer run. My daughter and I cleaned up the mess. A built-in oak cabinet that housed all my music and was great for all kinds of other storage somehow survived. With careful cleaning and an application of lemon oil, it looked as good as new.

The basement family room was now a large empty space with only the built-in cabinet and the surviving tile. Fortunately, the flood water had been clean and receded as quickly as it had come. On a lighter note, Vickie had taken a pail and dirty rags outside to rinse them off at the outdoor faucet. A reporter roaming the area saw her and spoke to her. When the local paper came out, the entire front page was Vickie —who had grown into a very attractive, tall, young lady—washing the rags in the pail. I teased her, telling her, "Gee, you are a cover girl."

Life returned to normal but not before my emergency fund was decimated by having to replace the furnace and the dryer. I was able to squeeze out enough money to get the basement waterproofed with a sump pump. The family room was no more, and my extra funds weren't enough to replace it.

In November, I began having some pain in my lower right side. My doctor ordered an ultrasound which revealed a walnut-sized ovarian cyst. I delayed the surgery until the end of February, after the holidays, much to my physician's disapproval.

Vickie brought me home after the surgery and stayed the weekend to help me. The second day home from the hospital, Julie called. Without making any inquiries as to my condition, she unceremoniously announced that she was coming the next day—with Dad. I was only partially ambulatory and recovery from the surgery was slow. I was plagued with fatigue and still woozy from the anesthesia. Despite all of it, I welcomed my father and did my best to settle into our old routine.

Summer arrived, and I decided to chance a four-day trip to the family home for July Fourth. It turned out to be a good decision: the weather was wonderful, and Dad relaxed on the porch as former students stopped by to say hello and share school memories. Julie and I loved seeing so many people express their appreciation for our father. Some days our house was so full of visitors it looked as if we were having some sort of family reunion. Dad was warm and cordial, though later he said that he didn't care whether folks visited or not.

When we returned to my home, Dad confided that Julie was taking things out of his house. I had heard such allegations before, even from my mother, who had tried to warn me before she died. I was never certain whether to believe it or not. I thought that the items were likely just misplaced, or, at worst, Julie was removing items already promised to her.

The next time I saw Julie, I told her what Dad had said. Julie shrugged and said, "He must have misunderstood." I trusted my sister implicitly and felt sure that, with the ethics we had been taught, she would never do anything dishonest or unfair. There were certain cherished items each of us had been promised, and I assumed, if she was taking anything, it was her intended share. After all, Dad had given her Power of Attorney—*or was it because he trusted Jim that he did that?*

* * * * *

Near the end of August, there was a horrific rainstorm north of my home that resulted in flash flooding over land. Once again, our quiet little stream became a raging, destructive torrent, spilling over its banks into the streets, yards, and basements. My basement began to fill with water. The city rushed to put sandbags in place along the streets and neighbors helped place sandbags against the foundations of the townhouses. The floodwaters easily breeched the sandbags and foundations of our homes. Finally, it reached the front porch top step, eight inches below the landing. Water rushed through my back door, cascading down the basement steps when the back door was inadvertently opened. Ironically, the sun was shining.

    I called Julie and told her of the dire circumstances. Dad did not want to stay at a shelter, and it wasn't at all clear if we would be able to stay in my home. Could she meet me halfway? I would get Dad when all was settled. The trip involved two hours each way for each of us. City workers paddled a boat up to my front door to evacuate us. Our six-day battle with the flood was lost. Vickie picked us up at the edge of the flood area. Julie was informed that my basement was filling with water, and I had to return as quickly as possible. When my father and I reached the agreed rendezvous point, there was no Julie. She arrived two hours later, acting as if nothing were amiss. I asked her what had happened to delay her, and she casually replied, "Jim wanted the oil changed before I came."

I said nothing more, just transferred Dad and his belongings to her car, with hugs all around, and quickly departed. I couldn't help but be struck by what different worlds my sister and I lived in.

The water in my basement was lapping at the ceiling. Outside it had breached the top step and was beginning to come over the landing. Two neighbors clad in hip boots knocked on my door and informed me that the prediction was one to two inches more, which meant the water would probably reach the first floor. They offered to elevate the heavier furniture on blocks and carry the lighter ones to the second floor. I was so grateful for their help. Eventually, that same day, police came to the doors of townhouse residents and urged us to leave. The power was out, but we were assured the National Guard would be present. That night, I stayed in a shelter. Victoria stayed with me. A week later, the water receded, leaving filth in its wake.

Vickie and I cleaned walls and floors of the basement until we couldn't clean anymore. A friend from the church scolded me for not calling her as she would have kept Dad, but she came to help us. She separated my music and spread it to dry on my dining room table, then determined what could and couldn't be saved. One of the counselors from my unit at work brought a rotary floor machine to re-wash and wax the floor, but not before he dismantled my now warped oak cabinet and hauled it to the curb for pickup. Fortunately, the water had not reached the first floor, only the ceiling in the basement. My only replacement this time was my washer. Now I had to apply for a FEMA Loan. Unfortunately, I was just above the cut-off for a grant and that meant I would now have three payments: the house, the furnace, and now a FEMA payment. To add insult to injury, after the clean-up I had some strange rash appear on my hands. I had worn gloves but at times the dirty water had gotten on my skin. The dermatologist diagnosed it as ringworm. With treatment, the condition cleared within a month.

We were soon informed that a flood prevention project had been put in place. There would be a "deep tunnel" installed under the street that ran past the townhouses and would drain into the river, taking care of the extra water. The noise seemed endless as well as the dust and dirt as they pounded away, removing the concrete in the roadway. Most of the residents seemed encouraged despite the mess.

When the project was finished, there was another heavy rain in our area as well as in the Northwest - a double whammy! Once again, the roadway flooded, but fortunately the water only came up to the top of the curb. Residents of the townhomes and the residents of the lovely homes across the street were once again pumping out. This time, I was spared and was so grateful that I had waterproofed my basement and put in the sump pump!

Once I had things in order, I phoned Julie to inform her I would, once again, take Dad and offered to keep him until Alison's wedding in early October. She agreed. As the wedding date neared, I was feeling restless and irritable, and I struggled to keep it under wraps. Certain people at work began to annoy me and even my father began to get on my nerves. I hoped some "alone" time would help.

Several weeks before the wedding, I rushed home from work one day to take Dad shopping. We both needed clothes for the wedding. I purchased a new dress and he got a new suit, shoes, shirt, and tie. I couldn't help but notice how frail he appeared. It reminded me of a shopping trip with my mother. She felt wonderful after her transfusion and looked quite good despite the stage of her illness. She wanted to go shopping, so we took her to her favorite store. She selected several dresses but had to sit down and rest between fittings as she was so weak. The dress she chose was light blue—the one she would wear at her funeral. When I looked at my father in his new suit, I wondered if that would be what he would wear at his funeral.

When we arrived in Williamsport, we were immediately rushed into the wedding rehearsal dinner. The wedding and reception were the next day. My hope was that this second marriage for my niece would be a happy and lasting union. Through all the activity, I was not feeling well and had to spend a day in bed before making the four-hour trip back home. I felt flu-like and fatigued. When I returned to work, the day shift became more and more physically challenging. I was having trouble sleeping at night. Consequently, by the time my shift was finished at 3:30pm I would go home to take a nap instead of playing the piano or indulging in some other relaxing activity. I would awake at 8:00pm in the evening, hungry and exhausted. My reasoning was that my body had never adjusted to the day shift and requested a return to the 3-11 shift as charge nurse. With the new schedule, I was able to sleep through the night.

*   *   *   *   *

In November, a month or so after the wedding, Julie called to inform me that Dad had contracted pneumonia and had been hospitalized. She kept me informed and it appeared he was not responding to treatment. Vickie and I drove to Julie and Jim's as often as we could. During the last phase of Dad's illness, Julie called and said she had walked into his room and heard him praying to die. When he became unconscious, he was moved to an intermediate care unit. The doctor informed her he would probably pass away in his sleep and Julie phoned me to tell me there was no need to come. Dad passed just before Christmas. He had lost the will to live after my mother died and suffered unyielding grief for three years.

I had kept Dad with me a little longer that year so he would be at my house near his birthday before returning him to Julie's. I had never been able to go home for either parent's birthday and I was thrilled to be able to be with him. The day we celebrated his birthday dawned warm and beautiful. We went to breakfast and then for a stroll, arm and arm, talking and reminiscing. It was a special day and the happiest moments I had experienced in a long time. I was reluctant to take Dad to Julie's, and now he was gone.

In my grief I recalled what hardworking, devoted, loving parents my sister and I had. I also recalled some of my father's final words to me: "You know, your mother really thought you were something. Did you know that?"

I shook my head in the negative.

"She felt," Dad continued, "you were an honorable person and that you had a great sense of fairness. She loved your assertiveness and forthrightness. Most of all, she loved your generous heart. She always felt you were so in tune with our physical ills. You never overlooked or ignored our complaints and always made sure something was done about it. We talked it over and wanted you to have the car."

I was stunned and speechless. Dad had just given me the greatest compliment of my life, yet I wished Mom had told me herself. She used to speak of Julie fondly, and I knew she loved certain strengths in each of us, but I never was sure what attributes in me she loved most. I knew Julie was admired for her charm, her fun-loving qualities, and her talent for handling our mother when she became upset. Emotionally, I was more like Mom and did not do as well when she was upset.

At one point during the previous summer, Dad mentioned that he wanted to get the car signed over to me before he passed. He begged me to do this. I had told him I needed money more than a car. Dad became upset, saying that I didn't have to pay him for the car. "Take it! It's yours." he said. "Your mother and I both wanted this."

"What about Julie?"

"She understands," he replied. "She knows you need the help. You will get your half of the money." I finally agreed. This would allow me to sell my older car and have a nicer, newer car. The necessary paperwork had not been done as there had been the rush of yet another major flood. I felt all would be well, however, as Dad had spoken to Julie about it and this family lived by their word. Our word was our bond. Julie could be trusted.

THREE

MORE OF THE SAME

1987

Before my father passed in late 1987, I had been getting the flu every five or six weeks and was grateful I wasn't due for another bout. Vickie and I had a long journey ahead to attend my father's funeral. Thankfully, Vickie offered to drive.

Vickie drove without a break until four hours into the trip. We stopped for coffee and then took a short, twenty-minute respite. As we started out again, I could see my daughter was fading but she insisted she was okay. After another two hours, she finally admitted she was exhausted. We stopped at the next rest area and changed places. We were just under a hundred miles away from our destination, and I felt sure I could survive that long to get us there.

As we came off the expressway around two in the morning and made our way through the last major city before my hometown, there wasn't much traffic at that hour. Immediately, Vickie fell asleep, sinking deeply into her reclined seat. Checking my speedometer as I often did as I had no cruise control, I was hovering consistently at around 65mph. The road was clear, and everything around us was deserted, dark, and quiet as we proceeded to drive through rural farmlands.

We passed towering trees, barns, and older homes whose faint silhouettes stood out against a darkened sky. Only yard lights illuminated the barnyards. The air had a freshness, a characteristic of the Great Lakes, and I rolled down the window to take some deep gulps. After approximately twenty-five miles, a police car appeared behind me, a siren screeched, and a voice boomed: "Stop the car. Pull to the side."

Where had he come from? The road had appeared deserted. I pulled to the side of the road as instructed. A man with a flashlight walked up to my car and demanded I roll down the window as he aimed the light into my back seat. Cautiously, I rolled down the window but only a quarter of the way. Thankfully, my doors were locked. With the flashlight in my face, I could not see much but managed to observe a badge on a striped sports shirt.

Instead of the type of cap police officers wear, he was wearing a Stetson-type hat. As the flashlight wavered a bit, I could finally see he wasn't wearing a uniform. Fear coursed through me. He shined the flashlight into my face and said, "You were going ten miles over the speed limit. I have been following you for the last twenty-five miles. "Please step out of the car."

Who was he? Could he be a deputized, small-town marshal? I didn't have the presence of mind to ask. Also, I knew I wasn't going ten miles over the speed limit, I never drove that fast, and wasn't even sure my car could survive hard driving. If he had been following me for the last twenty-five miles as he claimed, he must have been driving with his lights out as I noticed no car behind me. Before I could respond or move at his command, Vickie suddenly awoke and sat up. Quickly, he raised the flashlight and the beam caught her full in the face.

Suddenly, he backed off and changed his tone of voice, no longer demanding I step out of the car. He said, "Slow down and drive safely." He walked back to his car, and I started out again. I breathed a sigh of relief as I observed him doing a U-turn on the highway and heading back in the direction of the city. Thankfully Vickie had been with me.

In my rush to get to my father's house, reporting the incident to the police never occurred to me. Brad later scolded me for not doing so.

We arrived at the family home at four in the morning. Julie met us at the door.

"Well, I guess it's first come first serve. You will have to sleep in the little back bedroom."

That meant someone was sleeping in my lovely, spacious bedroom. Liz and Josh were there as well as Alison and her new husband, Dan. I fell into an exhausted sleep amid Vickie's complaints about her aunt's behavior. I awoke nine hours later. Julie and Jim had handled all the funeral arrangements before my arrival.

The following day, we prepared for the visitation. It was a time when family members we didn't get to see often would come to offer their condolences. Students who remembered my father once again paid their respects and shared stories. At the end of the day, my exhaustion was so severe that I fell into bed, unable to socialize with my sister and nieces as we had always done before. Grieving my father was painful, but the emptiness that I had sensed in him after losing Mom had always been palpable. My pain was dulled as sleep overcame me.

The day of the funeral dawned cold, with a clear, radiant sun incapable of melting the snow that covered the ground in late December. We said our final goodbyes at the graveside, clad in heavy coats, scarves, and gloves as the crisp air forced the blood to our tear-stained cheeks. Dad had gone to the great beyond to be joined with his Abbie and reside with Him, who promised the thief that "today you shall be with me in paradise." Somehow, I knew Dad was at peace.

After the funeral, we spent a few days writing notes and just spending time together, but I couldn't help yearning for the way of life as I had always known it. I felt orphaned.

Vickie and I left for Williamsport. Christmas was only two days away and we would stay in Williamsport for the holidays. As I drove along, my daughter was quiet during the trip and seemed uneasy. When I asked what was bothering her, she answered with a question: "Why did Aunt Julie put you out of your bedroom?"

I shrugged. "She said it was first come first serve, and I suppose everyone just drifted into a bedroom to sleep, not giving much thought as to whose room it was. It really isn't important. The important thing is that we had a clean, comfortable bed."

"I don't like it," Vickie replied. "We have always slept in that room, and Aunt Julie knows it! She wouldn't like it if someone just 'drifted' into her bedroom and she had to sleep in that tiny back guestroom!"

Half amused by Vickie's reaction but feeling she needed a broader perspective, I said, "You need to try to be flexible and give others the benefit of the doubt. They use the house a lot when we aren't there, and probably thought nothing of it. There was no intent to insult or hurt us. It just happened."

Vickie shot me an exasperated look. "She never would have done such a thing if Grandpa was alive." She said no more but later complained to Brad about it. I still believed my daughter was overreacting. Little did I know how prescient she was.

FOUR

A DOWNHILL SLIDE

1987 - 1988

Vickie and I spent Christmas Eve at Julie and Jim's. We were all subdued on what ordinarily would have been a festive occasion.

We returned to Summerset on Christmas morning as I had to be at work at three that afternoon. A week later, on New Year's Day, a couple of hours before my shift, the phone rang and when I turned to answer it, I was seized with severe, paralyzing back spasms. Vickie drew a hot bath and called work, telling the supervisor what had happened and that I would be there as soon as I could. I arrived at work two hours later and by that evening was in excruciating pain, unable to sit comfortably or lift my arms to answer the phone. Finally, the supervisor was able to arrange for the night nurse to come in early. Holidays were difficult to staff. Vickie came to get me. As I struggled to get to the car, I thought of the terrible car accident back before my mother died.

The hospital where I worked was located on a four-lane highway and there were no left turn lanes into the hospital premises. I worked the 3-11 shift and rush hour had just begun. My car was small and lightweight, probably not the safest vehicle I could have purchased. As I signaled a left turn, I observed a car in my rearview mirror, coming up on me at a high rate of speed. I could see two heads close together: a girl, practically sitting in her boyfriend's lap. He was not paying attention! I braced for impact as a feeling of helplessness overwhelmed me.

The force of the impact when the car rear-ended me sent me just over the center line into oncoming traffic. Someone called an ambulance and the police arrived shortly thereafter. I was transported to the hospital where I was x-rayed and given a collar. The pain in my upper body and lower back lasted for five days before I returned to work.

I returned to my job at the unlocked drug and alcohol unit, still wearing my neck support. One of the psychiatrists was a small, slight man with a shock of black hair, a long face with a thin protruding nose and always seemed to wear brown. He was one of the most unattractive men I had ever seen but one of the nicest as I got to know him. I had seen him around the hospital, but he had never had a patient in our ICU, my regular unit. My first day back, he came into the nurses' station to get his patient's chart and mentioned to me that he had heard about the accident, adding that I looked miserable! He informed me he had been a chiropractor before becoming a doctor and in a gentle manner ordered me to remove my collar and sit on the floor. The nurses' station was not like any other in the hospital in that it was like a spacious living room with a large table and comfortable chairs where one could sit and chart. There was plenty of room to sit on the floor. I did so and removed my collar. He got behind me and cracked my back. Miraculously, the pain and all the discomfort disappeared. He told me the effect would only last a few hours and that I should probably have the maneuver done periodically to keep me comfortable.

My pain was allayed throughout most of my shift but returned later that evening. Four years later, with three protruding discs, I would begin therapy which lasted for ten months.

One day a man I hadn't seen before

approached me on the unit. He was a kindly, medium built 70-year-old man who was slightly taller than my five feet four inches, had thinning snow white hair, stunning blue pools for eyes and his face was pink and cherubic-like. He looked like a man totally at peace with himself and introduced himself as Gabe. He said he had heard about the accident and asked what insurance the man had. When I told him he advised me it was the worst company and that he carried that insurance when he was drinking. His words were, "Honey, keep a daily detailed record of your symptoms to show how this accident has changed your life." I did as I was told and chronicled my slow loss of function over the next nine months but never saw him again. The incident was forgotten until some seven years later.

After Vickie and I returned from Dad's funeral, my flu symptoms began to erupt every five weeks or so. I suffered mouth sores so severe that pain radiated down my neck, and my lips would swell. Slowly, I found that oranges, apples, sugar and alcohol could no longer be tolerated, and I had developed a gluten intolerance.

* * * * *

Two months later, in February of 1988,

I was awakened one night at 2:00 am by severe pain in my lower right side. Unable to walk, I called to Vickie, who had stayed for the night and was asleep in the adjacent bedroom. Vickie guided me down the steps to the first floor by having me sit on the steps and lower myself, one step at a time. She pulled the car to the side door and guided me onto a desk chair with wheels. She somehow managed to get me into the car. At the hospital, a battery of tests was done—all negative. I returned home and stayed in bed for the next several days. I assumed it was the flu again.

In early March, Julie phoned. Struggling with my health, I had only spoken to her once since Dad's funeral. She sounded distant on the brief call, only asking to be representative for our father's estate. Mom and Dad had named someone else in the will, but Julie explained that all had changed, and family members now took on the task. She added that she needed the money. That struck me as odd because Jim made great money in his managerial position and was also a licensed stockbroker. Still, I gave my sister the benefit of the doubt and said, "Okay."

There was no more communication between us other than I received the necessary paperwork to sign over my sister as executrix.

By spring, my general condition had slowly worsened, and it seemed any exercise caused me to have a flu-like illness. There were days I was unable to get out of bed to attend the physical therapy sessions due to overwhelming fatigue. I suffered from sleep disturbance, headaches, a constant sore throat, pharyngeal and body aches, stiff eye muscles known as "viral eyes", occasional diarrhea, loss of appetite, and chills. The "flu" now occurred every four weeks.

Julie called again in April and asked to transfer Dad's probate to her county as it would be more convenient for her. I consented, not considering the legality of the move as I trusted my sister and my brother-in-law.

My mental faculties were suffering due to my deteriorating condition, but a few things slowly occurred to me. Julie and Jim went to the hometown area monthly to visit Aunt Beckie as well as Jim's mother. Wouldn't that have provided sufficient time to get the work done in a timely manner?

Julie said that she had spoken to a probate attorney in Williamsport, and he had informed her that it was not in my best interest unless there was a lot of trust between us. Julie said she had assured him there was, but he still seemed reluctant. However, he also knew Jim had an impeccable reputation in the area's business community, so he agreed. Also, Julie asked if she and Jim could keep Dad's car for a while before I took possession. "We need an extra car for convenience when we are at Dad's place." I gave my consent.

* * * * *

It was June before Julie, once again, communicated with me. Finally, she called and asked if I was coming for July Fourth weekend. I assured her I would be there if my health permitted. She did not inquire about my condition at all.

In July, Vickie, Brad and I travelled from Illinois but in separate cars. My daughter and I went to my parents' home and Brad went on to his family's farm. Jim and Julie had already arrived at our family place, and everyone was settled in. They had settled into my parents' bedroom, Alison and Dan were in the guest bedroom, and Liz and Josh were in my old room. Once again, Vickie and I were assigned to the small back bedroom.

The following morning Vickie was angry at the sleeping arrangements. She packed and quietly left the house, telling me she was going to her father's farm. "Just tell anyone who asks that I like the shower at the farm better," she said. My parents' place only had a tub.

When Julie gave me a quizzical look as Vickie went out the door, my response was that she wanted to be with her dad. I was comfortable in the back bedroom, and that was all that mattered to me. The mattresses were newer than any others in the house, except Mom's special bed that she had bought due to her discomfort after she developed leukemia.

This Fourth of July visit gave me a chance to visit with my beloved Aunt Beckie, my mother's sister, who lived only a block away. We spent hours talking over old times as I had spent the eighth grade and high school years living with her after my uncle passed away. We spent a lot of time going over family Victorian, antique photos and my aunt had many stories to tell. She wanted me to take the pictures because she knew I planned to create a formal family history for the family. There were so many beautiful portraits from the 1800s, pictures of our greats and great-greats. I left them with Aunt Beckie as I felt my sister and I should go through them together.

The following day, Julie announced there was trimming to do to the yard bushes. The place was overgrown as Dad had done nothing at the house, even before Mom's death. Julie called out to me as I was taking a nap. I roused myself with difficulty and went outside to help. After picking up branches and hauling them to the burn pile for barely an hour I had to stop, depleted and simply unable to go on. I returned to my bed. Later, my niece Alison told me that Julie had complained about how little I helped with upkeep of the house. Stunned and hurt, I informed Alison that I had felt ill for some time now and that I was doing all I could. Alison replied that she and Dan used the house more than I, anyway, and that she herself hadn't helped with the trimming and her mother had offered her no criticism.

Later that week, as we sat around the table after dinner drinking tea, Julie informed me, "You should always let me know when you are going to arrive so we can be here. How long are you going to stay?"

"Just a few more days. I haven't been feeling well and hope the extended rest will help me."

Julie looked away disinterested in what she may have felt was my attempt to make excuses for not doing more in the yard.

"How long do you plan to stay, exactly?" she persisted.

"Another week."

"Then Jim and I will plan to stay as long as you do."

Was Julie being companionable? It was pleasing to be able to spend more time with my sister.

At the end of the extra week, Julie and Jim invited Brad, Vickie, and me to stay a few days at their home on our way back to Illinois. We did stop briefly on our return and Julie and Jim were cordial, as usual. During this visit, Jim showed Brad a large book that had belonged to Dad, published in the 1800's, about the county they had removed from our present home. Later, I would learn it was worth $2,500.00 because it was in mint condition. It was never returned to the house. Julie showed me a large, gray crock with a top that she had removed from the house. I was puzzled but did not pursue it. It was unsettling to see this, and I wondered if Julie, in her role as executrix, had the right. It did not occur to me to ask Brad about probate procedures. He offered no reaction to Jim and Julie's acts of "show and tell." I concluded they must be acting with transparency and earnest.

During this short visit, my sister was wearing a gold, antique wax seal necklace with a small cameo that had been Mom's. My thoughts were slow, and I couldn't respond in a tactful but questioning way as I normally would have. Julie noticed me staring at the neckless and I never saw her wear it again.

On the trip back to Illinois, Vickie began to complain, once again, about her Aunt Julie. She insisted that she acted as though she owned the house. "Can't you see that?" she said. She complained that so much had changed since her grandfather's death. From that time on, Vickie refused to stay at the house on July Fourth.

In August, I sent Julie a birthday card and also phoned to offer best wishes. She never reciprocated, either for my birthday or just to be sociable.

FIVE

PROBATE BEGINS

1988 - 1989

As summer turned into fall, my condition continued to deteriorate. I tired more easily; all my old energy gone. I lost weight, a few pounds at a time, my memory dimmed, and I found it more and more difficult to assess situations and make decisions. If I tried to recall past events, my head would pound. I attributed it to a "lousy memory." Unaware of how dull I had become, there was no awareness of the way I was. My income was now high enough that I could quit the extra shifts, and I hoped the change would slowly return me to good health.

By November my lip and mouth sores were so severe I was taking Tylenol daily. Deciding enough was enough, I made an appointment with a medical internist— a robust, pleasant man whose boombox voice could be heard in the waiting room.

He checked me over and did bloodwork. He told me I had pernicious anemia, adding that he wasn't going to treat it and wasn't going to do the defining test. "Take better care of yourself," he told me. I told him I was a health nut and always tried to eat a balanced diet and exercise, but he was impervious to this bit of personal information.

The time came when the "flu" began to recur in three-week intervals. I suffered severe abdominal pain on my right side that made ambulation impossible. I made one more ER visit that year, but all tests continued to be negative.

I discussed my illness with Vickie as she had some of the same symptoms but not as severe. My daughter had never been able to work full time but coached competitive figure skating. This worked well for her as she was able to set her own hours and she seemed to tolerate the rigorous schedules that were always a part of the competitions. She taught with a woman named Della, a former National Champion of Switzerland who now coached competitive figure skating. She considered Vickie a gifted teacher.

At three years of age, Vickie had contracted chicken pox followed by a red, swollen ankle joint. The pediatrician hospitalized her, but she returned home limping over the next six weeks. From then on, she would complain of stomach aches after eating certain foods. Always a lively and chubby girl, she became lethargic and thin. At times she ran a low-grade temp and her eyelids appeared swollen. Later, she often had to be home-schooled due to her chronic condition. Sometimes she would projectile vomit or have diarrhea when engaged in play or other physical activity. Despite all this, she wanted to skate and take lessons.

Brad and I talked it over and decided that since school was such a struggle, we wanted her to feel successful at something. We were puzzled over our daughter's academic woes as we both had been good students. Fortunately, Vickie turned out to be a gifted skater and won first at many USFSA competitions as a child. However, there were problems. She could not tolerate the 5:00 am practices so the only time Della required that was for testing. At these times during ice makes, she would lie down on a bench and sleep while the other skaters engaged in lively chatter. For the next four or five days all her symptoms were more severe plus her throat was extremely red and when cultured yielded nothing. When I took her to her pediatrician, he told me that I was the problem and not Vickie. "There is nothing wrong with her," he said with annoyance. "Just send her to school!"

I changed pediatricians and the new doctor told me there was definitely something wrong, but she didn't know what it was. She promised to treat her symptomatically. To my overwhelming relief, the interventions she tried were helpful. At age fifteen, Vickie was given a smallpox vaccination, ran a low-grade fever and didn't feel well for nine months. The pediatrician advised that she should never be injected with any virus again.

Vickie was able to progress through her gold figures. Strangely, she could never "see" her figures, could only "feel" them. The freestyle was a problem because of her poor energy level. She had begun to grow taller, and height was not the best for jumps. She did manage to test and receive her silver medal. Later she coached a student through her gold medal, then she was considered to have a gold medal. All in all, it had been a rewarding endeavor for her.

*　　*　　*　　*　　*

I didn't hear from Julie from August, when I had mailed her birthday card, until December, when she called and invited Brad, Vickie, and me for Christmas. Brad declined as he had other plans but followed us to Williamsport before leaving for his own holiday. He stopped in to say hello on his return and followed us back to Illinois. Vickie continued to complain bitterly about her Aunt Julie's conduct the previous summer. After I told her to try and just enjoy the holiday with her family, she appeared more resentful of me.

In January, I called Julie and thanked her for the lovely time. After the holidays, my condition continued to go downhill. Even with permanent charge duties back on ICU, I was no longer able to make frequent trips around the small 12 bed unit. I could sit and do my paperwork, but the range of charge duties were becoming difficult. Headaches escalated and were so severe they prevented me from sleeping for three days at a time, causing me to cry in utter discomfort and frustration. On weekends and days off, I would be in bed. Finally, unable to take it anymore, I made an appointment with a hematologist.

Once again teary-eyed, the phone rang and it was Sharon, my old and dear friend. We had grown up together and she had been a bridesmaid at Brad's and my wedding. We spoke on the phone from time to time and occasionally got together. She had even entertained Dad and me for dinner at her apartment in another part of the city but always declined to come to visit. We kept in fairly close phone contact, but Sharon had not been told about my developing problem. Finally in April, she was informed of the appointment with the hematologist. Sharon asked if Julie knew about this. I told her about my January phone call with Julie and added I had not heard from her since. An hour later, there was a call from my sister. Julie didn't say Sharon had called her, but that is what seemed obvious. My sister asked how I was, so I told her. I told her about Vickie's and my upcoming appointment.

Vickie and I went in for the appointment and I took my bloodwork report from the first physician. The hematologist was a small, kindly-looking man. He ordered the defining test for pernicious anemia, which was negative, and a week later diagnosed me with Myalgic Encephalomyelitis or Chronic Fatigue Immune Dysfunction Syndrome with a pre-leukemic blood condition. He didn't know if they were related, especially since my mother had died of leukemia, but he explained the anemia might be retractable. He said, "You aren't getting the flu, but you have an illness that has flu-like exacerbations." The treatment: rest for a time and gradually resume work if there was improvement. He told me it would probably be over in about two years, but the throes of the illness was just beginning. He confided he didn't know much about the illness—no one did. Then, he did something doctors seldom do that touched me deeply. He gave me a professional discount and would accept whatever my insurance paid for the battery of blood tests and all future office visits and bloodwork. My deteriorating mental condition and euphoria blocked my mind and emotions from overreacting to my dwindling finances, but I was struck by the doctor's kindness. Vickie wasn't feeling well either, so at the same time he tested her, and she was also diagnosed with ME/CFS. This explained so much about her, as to why she had never been like other kids. Later I was able to receive literature from the CFIDS Association which gave the ME/CFS profile for children and it fit Vickie perfectly.

Over the next couple of years, Vickie would have to stop taking her competitive figure skaters to competitions, as the widely varying practice schedules resulted in her spending three days in bed on her return home. She realized she could not manage a business with this kind of problem. Della had retired, so she made arrangements with other pros. They would take her skaters to competitions and do the early morning figures. This meant loss of income.

My recovery plan was to resume work on a part-time basis until I could resume full-time work. With Vickie out of the house and on her own, I decided to rent my townhouse and get a studio apartment until fully recovered.

My sister called and I told her about the diagnosis and my decision to rent the townhouse and use the little vacation time I had coming before asking for a medical leave. Julie invited me to stay with them during my medical leave of absence. Feeling hesitant and uncomfortable, I told Julie I would think about her offer.

Vickie went to visit her father and told him about my condition. According to my daughter, Brad's eyes welled with tears. He said, "Well, I guess we knew she was sick, didn't we?"

Brad and I had been divorced for fifteen years but had always kept in touch. He was my high school sweetheart, had always been there for me—even during my second, brief, disastrous marriage and during the flood, as well as any other problems that arose. Before the divorce, I begged him to go to counseling, but he had refused. Over the years we had become best friends.

*   *   *   *   *

My memory continued to fade, and my head pounded. The distant past remained a grey fog. Julie called several more times and urged me to come, "We might never have this opportunity again, and it would be so wonderful. Please, please come!"

Slowly, I succumbed to Julie's charm and accepted the invitation. There was no doubt in my mind that I would enjoy their beautiful home and hospitality. Julie said I would have to pay them room and board. The plan was to go to Williamsport as soon as my home was rented. I would come up with the amount Julie asked for from my meager income.

I informed the hospital of my condition and requested medical leave. I had gotten through the first few months working and trying to get my house ready to rent by drinking coffee constantly and taking Tylenol to stay comfortable. Sometimes I had to stay in bed, completely unable to function.

A few weeks later, Julie and Jim arrived at my place unexpectedly. Apparently, Jim had business in a nearby city. They were amazed at the watermarks on the basement walls. Although they had been told the extent of the damage, the visual confirmation was obviously shocking. I couldn't help but feel they were not in touch with the trauma of two such floods in two years.

As Julie was leaving, she said, "Oh, by the way, the Bluebook value of Dad's car is $2,995."

Stunned, I replied, "Why are you telling me this? If I have to pay for the car, I don't want it." I recalled pieces of my conversation with Dad four months prior to his death. "My understanding with Dad —"

"You don't have to pay for it," she said. "I am just telling you so you will know what the value of the car is."

Why would anyone want to attach a price to a gift? Julie said no more and looked away. We bid each other an affectionate goodbye. Later I would discover that Dad had requested that she send the title to him, but she had never done so.

I cleaned my hardwood floors to remove stuck pieces of padding before they were to be sanded and varnished. I painted my laundry room floor with oil-based deck paint. The odor caused me to exacerbate. Brad took some vacation time and painted the walls throughout. Many times, while working alone in the basement, exhaustion caused me to lie on my new carpeting in the newly finished family room until there was enough strength to climb the stairs.

I had sold my car the previous spring and planned to get another one as soon as I recovered. In the meantime, Brad offered me use of his old car. With the money from the sale of my vehicle, I was able to install much needed thermopane replacement windows in my home.

With my small savings, added to the money received from my father's estate, I paid for a two-car garage, finished the family room, replaced the dryer and added a FEMA pump with the FEMA loan. The pump not only stopped water coming in from the street that came underground and caused pressure on the foundation, but it also stopped any residual water from entering the basement and allowed showering, washing clothes and using the dishwasher during a flood. With all the improvements, I felt sure the townhouse could bring top rent and, consequently, there would be a small income over and above my mortgage and FEMA payments to help pay for Julie's room and board. This would make my survival possible until my return to work.

With all the details to take care of and my memory problems, it never occurred to me that Julie had never given me a financial accounting of our father's estate, nor did I think to ask for one. In Michigan, probate lasted nine months to two years, including disposition of house contents. It was now almost two years since Dad's death. Julie had not explained any rules of probate to me as she should have, but I assumed the contents would be divided by end of probate.

As the date drew near for my medical leave, I continued to decorate and paint the townhouse, falling ill more often due to the increased activity. When I was ready, I placed a "For Rent" ad in the local paper and the first couple who answered wanted it. They wanted to sign a three-year lease as the man was doing a three-year residency in cardiac surgery. Scott asked about my condition after asking why I wanted to rent my home. He seemed somewhat informed about ME/CFS. He and his wife assured me they would take care of any problems that arose and not to worry. I felt so blessed. They did exactly as they promised and over the next three years took care of the townhouse as if it were their own.

Several weeks before my medical leave began, Julie called to inform me that the probate attorney had listed the car on the probate. I again repeated that if I had to pay for the car, I didn't want it. Once again, she assured me it was only a formality.

*   *   *   *   *

I heard rumors that the head nurse believed I was malingering. How could she have missed the pallor, the weight loss and the blood tests I had presented to her as proof about my pre-leukemic blood dyscrasia as well as a note from the hematologist confirming the diagnosis?

Each year on the first Friday of June, the lead psychiatrist in the hospital, Dr. Swanson, held a Pizzafest in a private room at a nearby Italian restaurant. It was his way of saying thank you for our work with his patients. My last day of work was May 31st, but the staff urged me to come. I promised to attend if I felt well enough.

When the Friday evening arrived, it took all my will power and energy to go. Thankfully, it was a casual affair with everyone in work scrubs. Dr. Swanson did not usually attend but, if he did show, he spoke to everyone, had a piece of pizza and left.

When I arrived, the group was

gathered around a table in a large, dismal back room with bland, empty walls and a bare wood floor—a stark contrast to the main restaurant. There was only a large table with enough chairs to accommodate everyone. By the time I arrived, the pizza had already been served and was rapidly disappearing. Everyone greeted me warmly, but I noted that Kyrie, the head nurse, wasn't there. When we finished eating, I noticed Mark, one of my best counselors who had quit several months before to pursue his Doctorate in Psychology had come for the party. He announced that they wanted to give me their last farewells. All the comments were kind and supportive, but the compliment that touched me the most was that they liked working with me because, on the days I worked, my shift was very organized and made their jobs much easier. Then they added I would be missed and hoped I would return when recovered.

As usual, someone had brought a boombox for line dancing. In previous years I had always participated, but this year I was incapable. Feeling terribly viral, energy-depleted, and needing to get home to bed, I excused myself amid the blaring music and started to take my leave. David, a temporary counselor who was spending a year with us, caught up to me just before I reached the door. He was a nice-looking young man, probably in his mid-twenties, slightly taller than myself with close-cropped blonde hair and blue eyes. We had worked together for almost a year but had spent three months alone together on nights and had many long conversations during those shifts. He was working on his Doctorate in Psychology and had one year until completion. Amid the noisy music he leaned in close to my ear and said, "There is something I must tell you. I loved working with you, and I loved our conversations. You were so open, warm, understanding, and compassionate. I know I will never see you again, but I will never forget you and I just wanted you to know."

Stunned, I tried to pull my thoughts together. After a moment, my answer came, "I had no idea." Trying to come up with something else besides that anemic response, I added that it had been a joy working with him and that I was touched that our time together had meant so much to him. He asked for a hug and I gave him one and left.

*   *   *   *   *

A social worker called three weeks before I was to leave for my sister's and inquired as to how I was doing. She informed me that another social worker had taken a leave due to ME/CFS and added that they missed me on the unit, that things "just were not the same now." I was touched by her call. She was not a close friend but someone with whom I had a working relationship.

Dr. Swanson had a huge practice and was well known throughout the country. Celebrities and their offspring were sometimes seen at the hospital. On some occasions, their limousines brought them to the hospital from the airport for a visit. All the doctors were pleasant to work with except one, Dr. Adderly, who just didn't seem as social as the others. He was a slender man with a head full of greying hair and glasses and had been recently divorced, I later learned. In looking at him, I was always reminded of an F. Scott Fitzgerald book I had read long ago and had never forgotten about someone with a "discontented face." It described Dr. Adderly perfectly and I chuckled every time I thought about it.

Dr. Adderly never spoke to me except about matters concerning his patients. Then suddenly he asked me out to dinner! As tactfully as possible I declined. He looked rebuffed and left the unit without further comment. Several weeks later staff had our monthly meeting with him to discuss the problems and progress of his patient. He then peppered me with questions about his new treatment. Never in all my years as a psych nurse had a doctor quizzed staff about new approaches!

Although I wished it so, that wasn't the end of my uncomfortable contact with Dr. Adderly. Late one evening he entered the ICU. No doctor except Dr. Swanson, on one occasion, had ever done so. Dr. Adderly checked a chart briefly then turned to me and sarcastically made several cutting and nasty remarks then quickly left. I never saw him again. I often wondered if I reminded him of the wife who divorced him. I had to conclude that he couldn't handle rejection.

Dr. Sheldon was Dr. Adderly's direct opposite. He was a tall, bespectacled man with reddish-brown hair, a husky build, a hearty laugh, and a twinkle in his eye. He was a former priest and was married to a beautiful, black-haired woman—a former nun—with gorgeous blue eyes and a dazzling smile. They had two children. Dr. Sheldon connected well with people and we, personally, were often on the same page. As I became ill and began to lose weight, no one had seemed to notice except

Dr. Sheldon. One day he came to me and quietly said, "I think we should talk."

Talk about what? I should have known he would notice. It was with surprise and gratitude that I accepted his kind offer to meet him for dinner and "bring a friend." Thoughtfully, Dr. Sheldon had chosen an evening that was on my day off. I tried to wear something to disguise my weight loss—a dark blue suit and a bright blouse to add some color to my pallor. I tried to cover my face with makeup, but even my hair was difficult to manage since I had become ill. It looked like a dried-out bush, a perm gone wrong, instead of the smooth, shining hair I used to have. When I worked, my hair was pulled back with a clip at the nape of my neck so the texture was not noticeable. Something a little different was in order, so I let it swing free down my back and chose a colorful band to keep my hair from overtaking my face. I asked my friend Bonnie, a psych nurse I had known for years, to come along. It would give us a chance to catch up.

We met at a restaurant called "Calypso." We arrived at a charming building with floor-to-ceiling windows and glass doors. The place was lit up like a Christmas tree. Colorful murals covered the walls and there were no booths, just tables. Soft lighting illuminated small bouquets on each table. The place was warm and welcoming. We found Dr. Sheldon sitting at a table waiting for us and he greeted us with that wonderful, warm smile. He remembered Bonnie from work and peppered her with questions about what she was doing now. We had an enjoyable conversation over delicious food.

Over coffee, Dr. Sheldon asked what was happening to me and I explained my illness. He was told of my plans to take a leave of absence and how that was being frowned upon by the head nurse who thought I was malingering, and I revealed how hurt I was that she thought that. He offered me words of encouragement saying that I was his favorite nurse and that he would miss me, was sad to see me leave and hoped I would return when well.

Vickie helped me pack and label boxes. Some furniture was going to storage and the rest was to go to Brad's house, where Vickie now lived. Six weeks later, approximately a year and a half after my father's death, my medical leave began. Vickie reluctantly drove me to Julie and Jim's home. Elated to have this time with my sister and touched by their thoughtful invitation, I had no idea what was to come.

SIX

RECOVERY

1989

Julie's and Jim's home was spacious and welcoming. Situated on a deep, beautifully landscaped lot, it was elegant and yet comfortable. Julie put me in the larger of the two bedrooms usually reserved for guests. The room was newly decorated and carpeted in soft crème. Julie would come to my room often during the day and sit on the edge of the bed. We would talk like old times. It had been recommended that I drink purified water, so Julie always made sure it was available, even if she had to run out at inconvenient times to get it.

That year, for the usual 4th of July visit to the home place, Jim made a bed for me in the back seat of the car for the trip. My nieces, their husbands, and a grandchild came as well.

Four weeks later, on my sister's birthday, I dragged myself out of bed and dressed for the occasion before joining everyone in the family room. The family planned to celebrate both my sister's and Jim's birthdays at the same time as they were only ten days apart. They would go to the country club and then return home for the birthday cake that Alison had brought. Not strong enough yet to accompany them, I said I would stay home. There was plenty of food to warm up in the fridge.

After I ate something and cleaned up, I was exhausted and returned to my bed. Sleep readily overtook me. Several hours later, the family returned, entering the house amid laughter and lively chatter. Alison came to my room to summon me, and I joined the group for cake and coffee at the kitchen table. Julie made her silent wish and blew out her candles. Alison took charge and cut the cake: my favorite, chocolate with white buttercream frosting. The lively banter continued and there were a few humorous stories before gifts appeared. I promised to bake banana carrot muffins, Julie's favorite, when I was feeling better.

Julie gave Jim some stunning neckties and the girls gave him a couple of gift cards for golf and car washes. Jim gave Julie a ring, a peridot with diamonds since jewelry was her favorite thing. The girls lavished her with her favorite expensive perfumes and creams. The evening ended on a high note and the nieces and their husbands took their leave. I couldn't get back to bed fast enough, falling into a deep sleep that lasted eleven hours.

The following day, Julie was all aglow because of the beautiful ring Jim had given her. She wore it all day long, with frequent attempts to let the diamonds catch the light over the kitchen table as she sat there, beaming. Jim seemed pleased with her reaction to his gift. I found it odd that a simple ring could elicit such rapture, but it gave me joy to see my sister so exhilarated.

Days later, Julie invited me to ride along to the market. I sat on a bench while she did her grocery shopping. The outings continued, and as my condition improved Julie took me somewhere several times during the week. Finally, I was up more during the day and in three months had gained some weight back. I began to dress and apply makeup. Occasionally, my sister took me to lunch at the country club. On one occasion, Jim joined us with a friend who had flown in for the day.

Despite these improvements, there were still downsides. I still had body aches and viral symptoms. My sister brought me some herbal remedies and I began taking them. My appearance slowly began to improve, but my energy was limited.

During this first phase of recovery, friends had sent me books on healing and boosting one's immune system. I learned about and then practiced visualization and meditation. This was as much a contributory factor in my steady improvement as any of the other measures.

Eating healthy made me feel less viral and gave me a little more energy. Severe exacerbations still occurred every two to three weeks. I still suffered joint pain, muscle spasms, and body aches but it was tolerable with more rest. Hot compresses and baths alleviated the muscle spasms.

If Julie and Jim had company, I had to move out of the guest bedroom into Liz's old room with an older mattress that was hard and uncomfortable. This aggravated my discomfort. By the time of my three-month evaluation for my medical leave, I knew a return to work was unrealistic. Julie agreed. In September, my interview with the administration was unsettling, but they reluctantly granted another three months medical leave. The next interview would be on or around December 15th.

*   *   *   *   *

It was an eventful summer. Julie and

Jim led busy lives. Julie's and my cousin and his wife came to see me, as they had heard I was ill. Company came from out east for a week, friends of Julie and Jim's.

Alison was to have a baby in the fall and, after six weeks off, she would return to work. She asked if I would babysit for her. I didn't know if I could. Julie urged me to do it and promised she would help. She had her weekly activities such as choir practice, bowling, or golf depending on the season, bridge and lunch with the girls weekly, but she said she would cancel all those engagements if I was ill. She urged me to ask Alison for the amount she would pay a licensed sitter, but I could not do that. Alison and her husband were struggling: her husband worked and went to school. The price was set, just enough to cover my payment to Julie.

I began to help around the kitchen as I developed a little more strength and began to feel better. The tea kettle boiled dry a few times, and things had to be watched so they didn't burn but I did not attribute it to my mental incapacities from the illness. Overall, I did fairly well in the kitchen. I baked and made soups from a wonderful new cookbook purchased prior to my medical leave. My sister and I enjoyed the soups for lunch and had a lot of fun tasting new textures and flavors.

There was a ritual at Julie's and Jim's, a five o'clock coffee hour when Julie made a fresh pot of coffee and one or both girls would sometimes stop by, have a cup of coffee, and chat before heading home. On Friday nights, the girls, their husbands, and grandchild were frequent visitors. It was a fun time as we all gathered around the kitchen table. The girls and I had coffee; their husbands had a Coke. On these Friday evenings, one got the feeling this was definitely Jim's night to relax after a hectic week. He had one or two cocktails before dinner while watching the news and Wall Street Week. Julie had several cocktails as well before she served pizza. It was an evening of interesting discussions and funny stories.

In September, Alison delivered a baby boy and after her maternity leave she returned to work. She would drop off the baby in the mornings on her way to work. Often, I could not get out of bed early as I felt too viral, so Julie took care of her grandchild until I could get up. At least twice a week due to sitter problems, Liz brought her little boy, who was four, but carefully asked her mother, not me. Julie was almost always unavailable to help on those days other than the early morning.

This required me to care for two children twice a week, the baby and David, who was adorable but did not like to mind me. Julie did not require Liz to pay. Occasionally, Jim stopped home at noontime and seemed to enjoy his grandchildren. He worked long hours, leaving the house before eight in the morning and arriving home around seven in the evening.

*   *   *   *   *

We continued to go to the old family home one weekend a month to visit Jim's mother and Aunt Beckie. Jim took part of his summer vacation too, so at times we were there for a week or more. I was able to spend time with Aunt Beckie and knew I would even get to visit her near her birthday in November, weather permitting. I had never been able to do that when I was working. At least something good was coming out of my illness.

In my younger days when I lived with her, we had been involved in musical activities. Rebecca was my musical, artistic aunt, and we shared many interests. She was also a very spiritual lady.

On one of my visits, Vickie joined me. Aunt Beckie, once again, went over the family portraits with us and tried to give them to Vickie and me. Vickie was willing, but I declined. I didn't feel right about taking all the best antique portraits of family members and felt strongly these things should be shared with my sister. We thanked Aunt Beckie for her generous gesture, saying we would leave them there for now. Aunt Beckie said she was afraid things wouldn't be there for me when I would be ready to take them. "Things are disappearing," she said. I discounted my aunt's words as I couldn't conceive of there being a problem. Aunt Beckie was ninety, and I questioned her judgment. I didn't realize I had lost mine.

* * * * *

After the first of the year, Jim and Julie would fly to California so Jim could be awarded for top sales in the nation. There was frenetic shopping for clothes for the trip. Julie was tall, slender, black haired and beautiful with a very aristocratic bearing and wore clothes well. She loved jewelry which accented her appearance. In contrast, I was smaller, attractive but not beautiful, and had light brown hair which was highlighted, dressed conservatively, mixing and matching to save money with only small touches of jewelry. Our appearances were as different as our personalities.

Throughout the fall, there were puzzling situations and occasional unpleasantness, but I said nothing. I was a guest, and besides, the good times far outweighed the bad. I couldn't handle and didn't want conflict. Recall was a problem and thoughts were so slow in coming. I was unable to respond appropriately anyway.

The first time I became truly perplexed over Julie's behavior was during a visit with Aunt Beckie. My sister came along and asked me to sit with our aunt while she disappeared into the bedroom. A moment later, she emerged holding a small box. Handing it to me, she asked, "Is this Grandpa's ring?"

I recalled that our maternal grandfather's ring was antique 18K gold, with a diamond, and this ring did not resemble it at all. I told her no.

"What are you doing?" I asked, unable to recall that the ring had been designated to me in the will and had been put away at the bank.

Julie averted her gaze. "I just want to know where his ring is," she replied.

Both of us were to inherit our parents' and Aunt Beckie's estates and our grandparents' jewelry had been in my late mother's and my aunt's possession. I didn't immediately question Julie's concern.

I shrugged. "Ask Aunt Beckie."

"She probably wouldn't tell me," Julie said. In my dull state, I never thought to ask why not.

Julie went back into the bedroom and began going through drawers. I followed her.

"Do you need to get all the family jewelry together for the lawyer?"

Julie ignored my question. We were out of our aunt's hearing. Suddenly Julie handed me our maternal grandfather's old pocketknife. I declined her offer of the shabby keepsake.

In late autumn we were at the family home, and I was lying on the couch in the living room. Julie and Jim were indulging in cocktails before dinner while she cooked. I could hear my sister's elevated voice coming from the kitchen but paid little attention. Julie was not one who could hold her liquor. One drink and she would slur her words and become combative.

All at once, she stormed into the living room, red-faced, and announced, "If you want the organ, you're going to have to pay for it! It is worth a thousand dollars—that means you owe me five hundred if you want it!" then stalked out of the room.

I was dumbfounded. I recalled our

mother wanting me to have her organ as I was the musical one in the family. Was it a gift? Or was I to pay? I had limited funds.

Fifteen minutes later, Jim approached me laughingly and said, "Julie was a little high on her price. The organ isn't really worth a grand. It is probably only worth six hundred. We'll give you three hundred for it." I didn't respond to his offer, thinking the less said, the better.

*   *   *   *   *

My niece Alison, who was my godchild, spent many more hours with me than her sister Liz and at times confided in me when we were alone. On one occasion, as we sat around the kitchen table, I spoke about the diamonds they were to inherit. Because of my sister's preferential treatment of Liz, I wanted Alison to be aware that her mother had been entrusted with two diamonds of the three in the family, so that each of the granddaughters would receive one. Alison appeared completely unaware. seemed totally uninformed about her Mother's request to me for the diamonds. Startled, I informed Alison about her grandmother's Indian jewelry and how pleased I was that she and Liz would someday have some very beautiful pieces. Alison looked straight ahead and in a monotone voice, asked,

"Have you ever wondered why Mother has the best of Grandma's Indian jewelry?"

"I assume it is because Grandma wanted to say thank you for the extra things Julie did for her and Grandpa."

Alison avoided looking at me and in a soft voice asked, "Do you think my mother is materialistic?'

"Do you?"

"I'm not sure." My niece sounded troubled as though she didn't want to but couldn't avoid dealing with what might be the truth.

"Yes, she is very materialistic, Alison, but then she has been surrounded by many beautiful things here in her own home. Your father has always showered her with valuables and many beautiful things, so I think it is inevitable."

Alison looked down, appearing despondent. "Why does my mother lie so much?" she asked. This conversation seemed very difficult for her but she apparently needed to discuss her feelings and concerns.

"Does she?"

My question was met with a long silence before she replied, "Yes, even to Dad. It upsets me."

"I suppose she is afraid to always be truthful. Perhaps it was our strict upbringing. I did not react that way because our parents were also very loving, but everyone is different." I could not recall any time in Julie's adolescence where my mother hadn't dealt with her behavior effectively.

"My mother thinks she is a positive person. Do you?"

I chuckled. "No."

"I don't either. None of us do. When we try to tell her, she refuses to believe us."

Beginning to relax, Alison continued, "I get into trouble if I probe or give an opinion that she doesn't agree with. I am not allowed to mention anything, no matter how wrong I think it is. She's hard on me, but I deserve it! She is never wrong, and she never apologizes. My mother is always right. She really is you know, and I believe that."

I was appalled. This was a married young woman in her early thirties. "No one is always right except God," I said.

I had witnessed Julie's accusatory and judgmental attacks on her daughters in the past, and my heart had especially gone out to Alison. Both girls were always extremely respectful to their mother and rarely defended themselves. Of course, Julie allowed no ongoing discussion if the views differed from her own. Silently, I began to think of my sister as the "Dowager Empress".

Vickie commented later that she didn't understand why Alison kept coming back for more abuse while Liz usually steered clear of her mother. My daughter would never have tolerated any such treatment from me. Our relationship was openly communicative and empathetic. Vickie could always voice her opinions without censure.

Some weeks after our first conversation, Alison brought up her mother and her intrusiveness. She related that Julie closely scrutinized the time she spent with me. After I had spent one evening at my niece's home, Julie probed her as to what we had done all that time and demanded to know what we had discussed. Alison told her we had talked about interesting medical cases involving allergies, as she had many. Alison said that her mother had sniffed disbelievingly. "Why is she like this?" my niece asked me. "It wasn't really any of her business, but I told her the truth and she didn't believe me."

I tried to be helpful in my answer. "Well, it really isn't her business, but you girls seem to tolerate her intrusiveness most times, so although this may be more noticeable and annoying, it is only a continuation of what she does. Doesn't anyone ever confront her? Sometimes, I have seen her be very inappropriate. Is it because I am here, and no one wants to say anything with company around?"

"Dad does," Alison replied, "but we aren't allowed to. Dad says what he has to say and then, for him, it is over, but not for Mother. For her, it is never over. She is unrelenting. My mother never apologizes for anything she has done. Liz complains about her too, and occasionally she has objected directly to Mother."

I suggested that Alison distance herself and discuss only superficial social matters. "She will only do what you let her do."

"I am going to discuss this with Liz because we don't know what to do about it. In all fairness to my mother, Dad can be dominating in some ways and tries to control her at times. I see her fighting that. Maybe she has to resort to certain tactics to avoid that control. I don't have the answer."

If Jim was dominating and controlling, I never saw it. In my presence he seemed docile as a lamb. I told her I had never seen him act in that fashion. We talked for a few minutes more, about her mother's favoritism with Liz and Alison's weak health. I sympathized with my niece, feeling sorry that she had struggled so all her life with allergies, asthma and low energy. She admitted she resented Liz because of the preferential treatment by her mother. "I try very hard not to resent my sister." I urged her not to resent Liz. It wasn't her fault. She agreed.

*   *   *   *   *

One afternoon, Julie had been out with her girlfriends for lunch and cocktails and had come home in time for the family coffee hour at five-thirty. Today, there was only Julie and me. We were sitting at the table holding our cups when Julie suddenly exploded: "You know, you didn't even keep in contact with mother. She didn't hear from you for long periods of time. She said you didn't call. You neglected her!"

I was struck speechless by her outburst.

She exploded again: "Mother wanted you to go to New York with her, but no, you had to go to New York with your friends instead of spending time with your mother!"

Bewildered, I struggled to find words. What was Julie talking about? I was entirely at a loss to recall the incidents so remained silent, unable to defend myself.

"I suppose you have spent all the

money you inherited from Dad!" she persisted. Then demanded, "Well, what did you do with it?"

"I used it to get the townhouse ready to rent so there could be a decent income while I can't work,"

"You have money! You have plenty of money!"

Was she referring to my small retirement fund? My savings had been decimated by medical expenses and the floods.

I left the kitchen. Somewhere in my foggy mind, a memory came to me: "When upset, leave the area."

Even amid such uncomfortable episodes, I still had some good times with my sister. My birthday was one of those times. A few days before my birthday, Julie informed me we would have dinner at the country club to celebrate. The surprise plans caught me off guard. Eating at the country club was always special, not only for the ambiance but the restaurant had an award-winning chef.

I took it easy when the big day arrived. I didn't want to be a limp dishrag at dinner. I rested after I showered, as even that activity depleted my energy. After I donned some nice clothes and applied some make-up, Julie, Jim, and I left for the club, where we'd be meeting the girls and their husbands.

When we arrived at the club, the girls and their husbands had not yet appeared. We were seated at a large table near the windows, facing the golf course. It was cold outside, with a light sprinkling of snow that glistened under the lights emanating from the club house. It looked like an oil painting. The room was dimly lit, and candles graced the table where we were seated. The softly lit dining hall gave me the feeling of luxurious relaxation. *How could one not enjoy this?* I found myself thinking.

Julie and Jim ordered their drinks before dinner. They each had a martini, and I had a Perrier with lime.

The girls and their husbands arrived a few minutes later.

I ordered salmon, my favorite, and was not disappointed.

Throughout dinner we had a lot of fun discussing funny incidents and sharing entertaining stories. Everyone seemed to be thoroughly enjoying themselves. When we finished and our plates were cleared away, the waiters and waitresses surrounded our table, setting pieces of cake at everyone's place, with my piece holding a candle. The staff sang "Happy Birthday".

On returning to the house, fatigue was setting in. I excused myself to my bedroom and as I was mounting the stairs a sharp pain shot through my knee. I held fast to the railing, barely making it up the steps. When I crawled into bed I fell into a deep, eleven-hour sleep.

*   *   *   *   *

Thanksgiving was upon us and Vickie called to tell me she would spend it with me. I was touched that she planned to drive all the way by herself. It would have been easier for her to stay with her dad. She arrived at Julie's on Thanksgiving Day —with her Norwegian Elkhound puppy. Julie tried to be gracious as she wasn't crazy about dogs. Vickie was not adept at handling the puppy quite yet, and in no time Sonia, the dog, was chasing Julie's cat throughout the house. In the pandemonium, both ended up in the master bedroom where the cat sat atop the headboard and hissed at the dog, who in her eagerness to get at the cat knocked over Julie's lamp. The shade looked a little battered, but Julie assured Vickie that it was alright and turned the shade in such a way that the damage wasn't obvious. I was amazed at Julie's tolerance.

At Thanksgiving dinner, someone

dropped their lacey napkin on the floor and Sonia chewed an end. Julie, again, tried to be gracious, but I could see she could barely conceal her feelings. Things were getting out of hand. I felt embarrassed, but Vickie often took exception to anything I said. I suggested Vickie chain the dog outside during the day and bring her in at night to sleep with us, if Julie agreed. She did. Vickie seemed agreeable but failed to apologize to her aunt.

My daughter slept in the other twin bed in the room I occupied. Just before we went to sleep, she commented, "Well, I see Uncle Jim has the knife you gave Grandpa!"

I had seen Jim using a red Swiss Army knife and thought it looked familiar.

"Well, it looked familiar," I said. "Besides, even if I had remembered, I wouldn't want to take it away from him. He likes using it."

"Mother! You are too soft! You paid a lot of money for that knife. What is Aunt Julie doing? Giving things to her family that we gave as gifts? Has there been a division of the property yet?"

"I'm probably too soft," I agreed, "but I don't want to fight over things. Probate is almost over, and I want estate business to go smoothly and fairly. There are some instances of mistakes, but Aunt Julie means no harm."

Vickie scowled. "They only think of themselves!"

"Well, maybe you are partly right, but they mean no harm or unfairness to me."

"Mother, you are so naïve."

"Vickie," I said, matching her tone, "you are so resentful! Bag it!" I turned out the light.

The following day, Vickie could barely conceal her resentment. On Saturday morning, the day she was going home, she asked me if I would go back with her. She explained she had to attend a small, one-day competition out of town for her skaters and needed someone to dog-sit. She had given me no forewarning. Alison and her husband had gone away for the weekend, so there was no way to make arrangements with them regarding childcare. I explained to Vickie that I was responsible for caring for the baby, and that Aunt Julie had a busy week ahead and couldn't be responsible either. Sympathetically, I added, "If you had just let me know ahead of time, it would have given Alison time to make other arrangements."

Vickie answered irritably, "Well, you could if you wanted to!"

"I have a responsibility to Alison, and that wouldn't be fair to her. You should have asked ahead."

"That's just an excuse!" she shot back. "Aunt Julie can inconvenience herself a little. You are my mother, and I need you with me." With tears in her eyes, Vickie kissed me on the cheek and left. I felt sorry she had come all this way to feel so rebuffed upon leaving. I made her promise to call when she reached home. When she called she sounded better and assured me she had gotten a friend to dog sit.

Later, Vickie's words came back to me. Was I naïve? Was there something amiss? I couldn't conceive of it. I was blissfully unaware that I should have been informed by the Representative the rules of Probate and the process of division that should have already taken place.

SEVEN

DIVISION

1989

We were nearing the end of the two-year probate period. I assumed Julie would signal when things were in order and it was time to distribute designated and cherished items.

Over the previous summer and fall, Julie had said I could go through my mother's costume jewelry, which was still at our parents' house. I could also have our mother's stationery, old scarves, and gloves. I was firmly instructed I was not to touch anything else. My assumption was that Julie was preparing for division. We both agreed we should remove gifts we had given our parents and promised porcelain items, if we wished. I was unable to recall much of what I had given my parents. Nothing around the house jogged my memory. Consequently, I didn't remove much. I couldn't stand to touch my mother's costume jewelry as I was still grief-stricken. I would sob with each attempt and so I gave up trying to make choices. My mother had loved big, colorful bracelets and pins with colorful stones.

During one trip to the hometown that autumn, I was on my way upstairs to bed when I passed Mom's China cabinet. It was in disarray, with shabby-looking pieces I couldn't remember being there. The beautiful Victorian pieces of our grandmother's had been replaced! Not a single one remained. I asked Julie about it and she explained she had removed pieces for safe keeping.

"When are we going to divide them?" I asked.

Julie looked away and replied with a tone of finality that disturbed me: "I just don't know."

My final thought as I climbed the stairs to go to bed was, *Is Julie going to cheat me?*

Days later, Julie discussed the disposition of my parents' house. Jim was there too. She informed me they needed to use the house as long as Jim's mother and Aunt Beckie were alive. She argued that Jim had said real estate prices were down and that they should wait until the market improved. She also insisted that Aunt Beckie would "just die" if that property was sold. Jim's mother lived eight miles away and she could have housed Julie and Jim, but not their girls and families. Selling our parents' house would have meant less expense for me. Aunt Beckie would have accepted it. Even in her old age, she had always been a flexible person. The simple fact that Julie loved the house and wanted to continue to use it at my expense escaped me in my love and trust of my sister. The money for upkeep was unaffordable for me. Julie urged me to agree on a joint deed so that the house would automatically go to either of us in the event of the other's death. "Jim and the girls don't want the house and, since I am older, I would probably die first—then the house would belong to you."

I felt even more confused and vaguely responded with, "I would sell the house. I wouldn't be able to afford it. I can't even afford it now when I am only paying half."

Jim began to laugh and looked at Julie, who laughed too. "No, honey. You girls should have tenants-in-common, the type of deed that would allow each family member to inherit their half share of the property on the death of the other." Jim's correcting Julie's assessment of the house situation puzzled me, and it would be a while before I would be able to understand the significance of that conversation.

Overall, the decisions made during this time were not made with any concern for my financial welfare and I was too ill to be aware of the implications of those decisions.

Later, Jim laughingly said he would take the house off my hands if I offered him a "real good deal." He proceeded to offer half of the assessed real estate value but didn't want to include the contents, which was valued at half the value of the house. In my normal state, I would have quickly come back with, "Now, Jim, you know I am the one who needs the good deals right now and your offer is not a good deal for me."

It was agreed furniture would be sold at an estate sale when the house was sold, but what remained were the small, valuable items, the cherished and designated items, and family memorabilia. When was that division going to happen? Julie continued to be evasive.

* * * * *

On one of my visits to Aunt Beckie's, Faith Lowery was there. She worked for Aunt Beckie cleaning, cooking, and checking on her and had done so for years as she only lived a block away. She had worked for my parents as well and was known to be an honest and decent person.

That day, Faith seemed troubled. She took me aside and told me Julie had come to her home and told her I had stolen a Nippon pitcher from Aunt Beckie's house. Faith told her that she had been at Aunt Beckie's the day she gave me the pitcher, along with some silver pieces. She confided that Julie, on a previous visit, had told her that I had the same condition as our mother and that I was going to die. I assured Faith that my blood condition appeared to be improving and might retract altogether, as there was a possibility it was related to ME/CFS. With my slow thought processes, I failed to connect Julie suggesting a joint deed to the supposedly fatal blood condition she believed I had.

On another occasion, Aunt Beckie requested that Brad should come to see her. He was at the family farm, hunting. Together, we visited Aunt Beckie. She asked that Brad take the Tiffany lamp, a 36-inch antique that hung in her dining room and had been purchased by my grandfather in an estate sale at a mansion in Cleveland, Ohio. Shocked at my aunt's request, I asked why, since Julie was to receive it. Aunt Beckie explained, "I am angry at her for the things she has done. She doesn't deserve it."

Brad declined, saying, "Don't involve me in this, Rebecca. Tell her how you feel."

Had Julie not been forthcoming with Aunt Beckie in trying to get certain valuables together? I wanted to give her the benefit of the doubt and get everything resolved without any conflict. Julie kept saying she wanted there to be no misunderstandings, but she was less than transparent.

On one of the visits to see Jim's mother and Aunt Beckie, I spent a long afternoon with my aunt. We reminisced and she expressed concern about my health. I assured her I was slowly improving. Then, Aunt Beckie became fretful and complained that she had signed certificates over to Jim for $4,000. "I am angry at him and Julie because they haven't brought me the money." Later, I mentioned the incident to Julie who said that, indeed, Aunt Beckie had done that, but Jim hadn't cashed them because she didn't need the money right now. I considered they were looking out for Aunt Beckie's welfare and would cash the certificates when they were needed.

Deeper into the fall season, my sister continued to discuss property and the probate. All cash I would receive had been dispersed, Julie informed me, but she gave me no written, factual accounting. Julie said the contents of the house were going to be estimated rather than inventoried. She said the man who estimated the value was able to give information on some valuable household items and told me that the large, "Gone With the Wind-style" ruby glass oil lamp I was to inherit was worth $400. Also, she said he estimated the organ at $1,000 and an antique Victrola promised to me at $250. Once again, I wondered why Julie was getting a price for what I felt were gifts. In my slowness what escaped me was that Julie attached no monetary value to her own designated items. She simply avoided discussing them at all.

On another occasion, Julie said they should sell the lakeshore property that our maternal grandfather had owned. Mother and Beckie had held it in hopes it would appreciate in value, but Jim and Julie recommended it be sold. Julie said it wasn't worth anything. "Why not? Lake property is always valuable." Jim explained that the area wasn't zoned and probably wouldn't be, which devalued it. Julie added that they had received an offer from a nonprofit nature association, and she had told them we would take it.

I became upset. "Why are you doing this? You didn't tell me anything about it. Can't we withdraw and advertise?" I was hoping that, eventually, as property edged higher this would be an additional source of cash for me.

"I don't want the county to continue collecting taxes on the property," Julie said, "because Mother went to court to get the taxes reduced. She won and the following year the county raised the taxes again. I am getting even!"

"But why didn't you ask me?"

"Do you want to pay the taxes?" Julie's voice rose in anger and she side-stepped my question. I knew I could not take on anymore expense, but it didn't occur to me to even ask how much the taxes were. Didn't Julie ever give any thought to my financial situation? Later, on one of my better days, I remembered my mother had received an offer of $10,000 but declined it as she was convinced lakeshore property would bring more. Julie sold the property for $5,000. As the value of property soared over the next five years, before the great recession I heard the adjacent property to my grandfather's lot sold for around $50,000 and larger lots for $90,000. Brad was appalled when he heard what had happened and said he knew someone who would have bought the property at that time without advertising for $10,000. I was simply too slow to deal with my sister.

* * * * *

December was a busy month as the family prepared for Christmas and finished their holiday shopping. Brad and Vickie had accepted Julie's invitation to stay for Christmas and the yuletide season was enhanced by perfect winter weather. After a few days of freshly fallen snow, the large, mostly modern homes on Julie's and Jim's Street looked as though they were nestled in glistening drifts of sparkling cotton. It truly was a winter wonderland. The beautiful scenery made the Christmas season even more festive. Julie had asked me to help in the choir at the church as they needed more soprano voices. The physical effort needed to project my voice and the practice required for me to get back into shape was a concern. I hadn't done any singing for a couple of years, ever since the beginning of my physical downhill slide.

My other concern was the physical effort of getting up early enough for the usual Sunday morning services and having the energy late enough in the day to do the Christmas Eve service and not land in bed with flu symptoms and mouth sores. Despite all my concerns, I consented to participate.

Christmas Eve morning, the choir sang

all the carols at the service. The house and tree had been decorated and, after church, we prepared homemade dressing and wrapped gifts. Alison, her husband and baby as well as Liz, her husband and son would all be there for Christmas Eve and the evening Christmas service. Earlier in the day, Julie and I had set the table, adding leaves to lengthen it and collecting chairs from throughout the house so everyone could be seated for dinner. As I helped Julie set the table, she brought out a beautiful, Irish linen damask cloth which we put on the dining room table. It looked hauntingly familiar. Julie stole a glance at me as we smoothed it over the table, but I dismissed the feeling as there was only the accompanying fog.

Brad and Vickie arrived early in the afternoon. By late afternoon, we began to get ready for Christmas Eve service. At the required hour, the family got into their cars and headed for the church. The service began with special music. The choir director had chosen "Hallelujah Chorus" and several other difficult pieces. During the service, the music went extremely well. The choir was elated. The men had outdone themselves and had responded to the choir director's cues even better than during rehearsal. An appreciative audience had a way of bringing out the best in those performing. After the service, the choir director asked me to join him at another church for his other service on Christmas Day. He offered to pay me, but I was afraid of my health not being reliable. I declined the very flattering offer, grateful I had been able to make it through the two services over Christmas.

After church, the family drove through the streets in their area to see "Venetian Lights", Christmas decorations, and the luminous light show. Jim drove us to the older parts of Williamsport, where there were majestically beautiful homes accented by gorgeous and lavish lawn displays, turning each home into a magical fairyland. I sat quietly in the backseat of the car and reminisced. From early childhood, our Christmases included both sets of grandparents and Aunt Beckie. This was so different, yet we were having an enjoyable and pleasant Christmas with only a tinge of sadness.

Earlier in the month, I had been very upset and cried because the weather had been so bad, we had not been able to make our usual visit to Aunt Beckie's and thus had to ship our gifts. I couldn't help feeling sad for my aunt, who had always spent the holidays with the family and was so alone now that Mom and Dad were gone. Calling her was a waste of time as she did not do well on the phone with her hearing aid. *Maybe we could make it to see her after the holidays...*

My sad musings stopped abruptly as we drove into the yard, and everyone piled out. The house was filled with the aroma of roasting turkey and, within an hour, dinner was ready, the table exquisitely set, a tribute to Julie's elegant taste. The atmosphere was festive and convivial. We had dinner amid bright chatter and laughter before adjourning to the family room, where we opened gifts.

Occasionally over the last few weeks, Julie had kept asking where my designated items of jewelry were. My memory continued to be spotty at best, with bits of information surfacing at times that would be lost again. Julie kept reminding me she needed to get all the missing valuables together. Finally, on Christmas Day, the China cabinet incident gone from my memory, I approached Julie and told her that my promised jewelry had been kept for me in a safe deposit box at the bank in our hometown. What I wasn't able to recall was why Mom and Dad had placed them there.

The day after Christmas, I asked that Jim and Julie visit Aunt Beckie after New

Year's, when I returned from my doctor's appointment. Jim agreed, stating there was too much snow and bad weather to bother going there. "No," he assured me "we will not be going to see her anytime soon."

Brad, Vickie, and I packed the car and headed back to Illinois in a severe snowstorm that did not let up, but we arrived home safely. My doctor's appointment was for January 2nd, though I should have gone around December 15th. The Christmas preparation and the fact I had a ride back rather than taking a train were reasons for the later appointment. I had finally begun to function about six hours a day, but knew I wasn't yet able to return, even part-time, to work. The hospital administration, I had been warned by friends who knew the situation, was looking for a reason to medically terminate me. They had never been understanding about the illness. I didn't know what I was about to face and worried about my medical coverage. In addition, my sister had her own plans for my future….

EIGHT

GOOD TIMES - PUZZLING TIMES

1990

Brad dropped Vickie and me at his home in Illinois and went on to Springfield. After spending a few days with Vickie, she dropped me off at my friend Sharon's. The time with Sharon was spent catching up on our families and our own lives. We exchanged recipes as she was a great cook and often experimented in the kitchen. We ate a wonderful dinner she had prepared for New Year's Eve. When it was time to retire, Sharon offered her bed and volunteered to sleep on the couch for two nights. I objected, as she had to work, and her couch was not a pullout. However, she persisted. She said she would be hurt if her offer was not accepted. Touched by Sharon's concern, my aching body appreciated the wonderful bed. We were asleep when the New Year came in.

I saw the doctor the day after New

Year's. Vickie picked me up, as she would have a checkup too. The doctor agreed to my part-time return to work but not until April or May if my condition continued to improve. The blood dyscrasia was almost gone for both of us. We left the office elated and drove to the Psychiatric Hospital for a meeting. When we entered the main lobby of the hospital, two of my former counselors met me with smiles and hugs all around. When was my return to work? They were informed that my doctor had advised rest for six more months. They were disappointed but gave me words of encouragement. When I met with Personnel, they informed me of the medical termination my friends had warned me about. The letter advising me of this had not yet arrived. Thanks to COBRA, there would be medical coverage for eighteen months, but the premiums would come out of my small income from the house rental.

*   *   *   *   *

Back in Williamsport, my sister and Jim revealed they had visited Aunt Beckie and Jim's mother in my absence. I was distressed at the news: *Why had they chosen to go when they did?* I asked Jim, who said Julie insisted on going despite the terrible weather.

They knew how upset I had been not to be able to visit Aunt Beckie for her birthday and for Christmas. The weather hadn't been any better for them to brave the four to five hour drive it took to reach the remote area during the short time I was away. I had not been to see my aunt since October. Why did Julie insist on braving the bad weather? It would be many months before I found the answer.

During the balance of my stay at my sister's, I tried to get Julie to have some kind of division of the designated, valuable, cherished items and family memorabilia (i.e., birth certificates, pictures, college diplomas, death certificates and marriage licenses). For the next three months Julie halfheartedly responded, trying to appease me. On one occasion, she announced that she had looked everywhere for certain items "but they simply can't be found. The seven antique demitasse silver spoons you were to receive are missing." These were our great grandmother's and had been given to our paternal grandparents on their wedding day. Julie had received her seven and, when our mother went to get mine, they were gone. Unfortunately, I thought the situation had ended there and could not recall much more to the story. My assumption at the time was they had been misplaced.

Pressuring Julie about my inherited items, her reply was, "I have looked everywhere, and your items aren't anywhere." I was stunned. What was happening? Why were all my things missing while Julie and Jim had everything that had been designated—and more. I broke down and sobbed. What was happening? How could this be? This was all I had left of loved ones, and now I had nothing. Julie watched impassively with no words of comfort or encouragement that they might eventually be found.

My sister tried to give the appearance of being more forthcoming and showed me a gold pen of our mother's, with her maiden name engraved on it, but took it away as quickly as she had produced it. Much later, I recalled it had been designated to Julie.

"When are we going to divide these things that you do have?" I asked.

Julie quickly changed the subject by showing me an antique, white gold, pearl and ruby necklace of Aunt Beckie's. She said that Aunt Beckie wanted to wear it at her funeral. Our aunt had told me the same. Julie added that Aunt Beckie had promised it to her. I wasn't certain Julie was being truthful, but as usual I wanted no conflict. Still, my trust was swiftly eroding.

On another occasion during these revelations, Julie suggested giving Brad Dad's everyday wristwatch. Puzzled and unable to recall what Brad had been designated, I shrugged and accepted for him—but something didn't feel right. Months later, Brad would verify he was to receive my maternal grandfather's shotgun. Only then would I finally conclude Julie was carrying out her own wishes rather than those of the deceased. At that time, I wondered what the duties of a Representative were. I had just assumed they were to carry out the departed's wishes. Was I wrong? It didn't occur to me to ask Brad.

Julie showed me our father's family's antique velvet Bible, which had ornate, gold-filled trim superimposed on the velvet and contained records of births and deaths. It was the most beautiful thing I had ever seen. Were we going to flip a coin for it? Julie did not answer, picked up the Bible, and quickly left the room. Later, I learned that the value of that type of Bible was five hundred dollars estate sale price. The show and tell continued, and one day Julie came into my room with Mother's pendant watch, a piece of costume jewelry that our mother had decided to buy so that I could receive the antique, gold-filled pendant watch of my maternal grandmother's. Of course, I had no memory of this. Upon seeing the pieces of costume jewelry, I asked if Julie had found what I was to inherit, unable to remember I had been told where it was by Mother and Dad and had given that information to Julie in one of my better moments.

"No," Julie said.
"What else is there to divide?"
"Not much."
"What is 'not much'?"
"Nothing, just nothing!"

The familiar feeling of treading on eggshells returned and I ended the inquiry. Probate had now ended some six months before. Later, Julie handed our mother's costume jewelry pendant watch to me. "Here, take it. It's very nice."

I still assumed I would receive what had been designated to me if it was ever found.

* * * * *

A few days after my return from Illinois, Julie said she had spoken with Sharon. She spoke firmly as one would to a naughty child: "You know, you left Sharon's front door unlocked when you left. It was unlocked all day until she got home from work. You really should be more careful what you do!" She looked at me with disapproval.

I struggled to recall events. I had not used Sharon's front door. She told me that a repairman was coming and to exit by the kitchen door, as it would automatically lock. Had I misunderstood these directions? It never occurred to me to call Sharon and clear up the matter, and Sharon never mentioned it to me in our later conversations.

As the March appointment neared, I felt more confident I could at least start back to work part-time, perhaps two days a week at first. Julie still didn't feel I was ready and urged me to take more time off. She and Jim even offered to let me rent an apartment they owned so I could work part-time and be near them in case it didn't work out. But I had to get away. There was an unidentified emotional discomfort.

I informed my doctor of my thirty-to-fifty-day cycles. I felt good and my activity level had increased. Sometimes, when I drove, my peripheral vision was distorted so I drove only when necessary. My blood picture was almost normal. The doctor gave his consent for me to work several days a week. It had taken a year.

* * * * *

Julie and Jim had monthly tickets to the symphony orchestra from fall to spring. My sister offered to take me to the April concert before I left. They were performing Schumann's "Spring", one of my favorites. Jim did not care to go, and she commented that she often had to invite a friend because he didn't care for the more classical performances. We managed to find something presentable for me to wear and I eagerly got ready.

We arrived at the concert hall and Julie pulled up to the front door for valet parking. My sister and I exited the car and entered the symphony hall. We had third row seats in the balcony, my favorite place to sit for concerts. The symphony performed beautifully, very much like the recording I had by the Cleveland Symphony. The prolonged applause and extra bows were well earned.

As we left, I was in high spirits. What a wonderful send-off this was. My life was about to change, hopefully for the better. Things were looking up!

NINE

A BRAVE ATTEMPT

1990

The first step was to get a job, so I applied at a hospital and was hired. Things were set in motion for my return to work. A friend urged me to take an apartment, though I had reservations about taking my furniture out of storage and all the expense. What if Julie was right and I wasn't ready? I knew I would have to start slowly.

Matt, my apartment hunting friend, sang and played the piano professionally at a club in town. Whenever I walked into the club, he called on me to sing duets, Broadway tunes, with him. What a voice and what a thrill to sing with someone who had appeared on Broadway. We became fast friends, a gay man who was kind and caring and a perfect fit for my life now that I had vowed to live. We helped each other out on social occasions, going as a duo when we needed to. For birthdays, we had dinner together. We had been friends for a long time. He argued I wasn't giving myself a chance under the best of conditions. Getting a place to live instead of renting a room was the better way to go. This way, he argued, I could cook for myself and not have to eat out. The doctor had seemed confident I would make it. Matt found a lovely apartment to sublease in a not-for-profit building, so the rent was extremely economical. The biggest expense would be moving my furniture. Matt took care of laying my carpet and chose the paint colors for the walls so that, when I arrived from my sister's, everything would be ready.

Before I departed for Illinois, a musician friend of Jim's had flown into town for the day. Jim thought I would enjoy meeting him. Julie had other plans so did not accompany us. My weight was back to normal, which meant I had my own casual clothes to wear, my color had returned, and I looked healthy. I was looking forward to the outing.

We were to have lunch at the country club. We arrived and were seated with our usual full view of the golf course. It was a gorgeous, sunny day outside. Presently, a pleasant looking, ruddy-faced, blonde, blue-eyed man approached our table and greeted Jim. Jim introduced me and after some idle chat we ordered. Eventually, the conversation centered on some tapes he had recorded of his music, and he inquired if I knew any agents in Illinois who handled musicians. I knew several and offered him some names. He was prepared to distribute his performance tapes and asked if I would be interested in helping him, but I declined. He inquired about the music scene where I lived and I referred him to some musicians who might be helpful. We finished our lunch and I wished him well.

Another thing that happened before I returned to Illinois involved my late father's car. Brad stopped in to see me and when he realized I was going to be using Dad's car he inquired as to when was the last time it had any maintenance. I didn't have any idea. Jim and Julie had driven the car from the hometown. Brad checked the oil and was immediately alarmed. The oil was thick and dirty. He volunteered to have the oil changed and check the other fluids. When Brad phoned Jim, he laughed and said nothing had been done for two years. Brad warned me that the motor might be ruined.

I left my sister and her family with gratitude and hugs for all. On the four-hour drive to Illinois, my father's Oldsmobile began to repeatedly stall. The car's red light began to flash and then every few miles the car would lose power and die. I pulled to the side of the expressway, as I sat there four youths in an old Cadillac on the other side of the expressway were staring at me! Because of my bad experiences on the road all my instincts were on alert. *Why weren't they in school or working?* Here was a woman alone on the highway without a cellphone. I was grateful it was daylight. Carefully the windows were rolled up and doors locked. Just as I feared the old Cadillac rolled up behind me and two of the four youths alighted from the car. They came up on either side of the car and walked around, carefully looking the car over. Then one youth did the talking through the closed window. "Did I need help?" I shook my head no while cautiously watching the youth on the other side of the car. He seemed to be observing the back seat which was empty as all my belongings were in the trunk. He wasn't carrying any obvious object such as a tire iron or even a flashlight but was looking the car over very carefully. The first youth asked if I was sure I didn't need any help, they would be only too glad to give me a lift somewhere. Emphatically I shook my head no and said, "No, thank you." They slowly walked back to their car and in a moment, they were gone. I breathed a sigh of relief.

Eventually, an older couple stopped to offer help. We managed to re-start the car and they led me to a service station several miles off the expressway. After an hour's wait, the station attendant looked at the car and could find nothing except the radiator fluid was low. I started out once again.

There were several more incidents where the car lurched and stopped. After a while it would start again. What should have been a four-hour drive became seven hours. Matt was anxiously waiting my arrival and had even called Julie to inquire as to my departure time. Amazingly, I felt only slightly tired from the long, stressful trip. I called Julie to tell her I had arrived safely.

Matt helped me settle into my new apartment, which was on the twenty-first floor with a view of the city. It had no air conditioning, but on hot days Matt insisted I spend the day in his cool apartment.

Grocery shopping was the next big hurdle for me. It was three blocks to the supermarket, then a walk through the store to gather the groceries, check out, arrange for the groceries to be delivered, then the walk back to the apartment. Soon, another old musician friend, Joel, was helping me with my grocery shopping. I sat and he shopped as I couldn't walk very far.

When Brad came to visit me, I told him of my constant problems with the Oldsmobile. He suspected the motor and radiator were finished. The car wasn't old, the body was in excellent condition, and it had always been garage kept. He offered to get it fixed. I accepted his kind offer, but when could I ever repay him?

"It's only money. Don't worry about it," he said.

Sadly, during this time, there was another flood at my townhouse. The flood equipment had malfunctioned. The shutoff valve had closed, keeping the water away from the house, but the sump pump had burned out. To my relief, the damage involved less than one inch of clean water so repairs would be minimal. Brad heard about this through Vickie and called me to insist that a new sump pump be added in addition to the flood equipment already in place. The new sump pump was larger and had a battery pack as back-up in case the electric power went out.

"I simply don't have the money," I said.
"I'll pay for it."
"I don't know when I can pay you back

and I already owe you for the car."

"Don't worry about it—it's only money."

Tears stung my eyes.

* * * * *

Re-establishing contact with old friends was a joy. Bonnie, Sharon, and of course Matt and Joel were wonderful to me. My daughter would also visit often. Brad would come into town on business once a month and sometimes take me to dinner. I was grateful for all the support.

I had a letter from Alison, who sent a lovely picture of Alex and thanked me for all the special care and music I had provided him. She said she felt her son had been given a wonderful start. That brought tears to my eyes. I missed Alex and lamented that I wouldn't be around much as he grew up.

As I waited to begin work, my flu-symptoms were on forty-day cycles. Elated, I felt even more sure of my goal to return to work full-time. My application for employment at a large general hospital with a drug and alcohol unit was accepted. I was required to take a math test and passed with a perfect score. I still had trouble recalling old memories, but otherwise my mental faculties seemed sharp.

Julie and Jim were in town on business at the end of April. They stayed for a weekend. I gave them my bed and I slept on the couch. To my surprise I was comfortable. We spent a quiet time together as I was to begin work the following Monday and didn't want to overdo.

Several weeks after their visit, Julie called to inform me that there was money left after probate and she was going to put all of it into a joint account to pay bills at the house. She explained that the money would pay off the sewer that the town had just installed. Jim had calculated that, at 2 1/2% interest, it would be better to keep the money to fund the house expenses. Julie said she would send me a card from the bank for my signature and Social Security number. The money should run the house for two years, which made me wonder why Julie needed to keep all that money on hand, but I refrained from asking as there would be consequences for questioning Julie's decisions. She also informed me that Jim's name would be on the account in case something happened to her. This would allow him to continue to take care of the bills. I would have to pay half of the taxes, upkeep, and utilities with very little backup money left from my savings. Julie ended the conversation by asking about my bloodwork. Joyfully I replied that it was the best it had been.

"Are you saying it's normal?" she asked.

"Well, almost."

"Good." Julie sounded matter of fact. Later, I received the card from the bank. I signed it and mailed it back.

One weekend Vickie invited me out to the house. Starting out with dad's car it stopped in heavy traffic. Petrified as cars sped by, I wondered *would the hazard lights sufficiently alert even the most aggressive or unobservant drivers?* A policeman appeared out of the haze of speeding cars, pulled up behind me and sat there until the car would start again. He followed for a short distance. I waved my thanks then he was gone. The rest of the trip was uneventful.

The job turned out to be more physically difficult than anticipated as the adjacent medical unit had merged with my unit a mere two weeks after I started. My position was medication nurse. On this large medical unit there were many PRNs — that is, extra prescription meds for patients to take as needed. I double checked all meds before giving them because my fatigue increased as the shift progressed. My position entailed walking up and down the halls many more times than necessary. I longed for the small, quiet unit where I had worked before.

*   *   *   *   *

In mid-August, after three months on the job, I had a sixty-day, symptom-free cycle, but the following cycle ended in thirty days. By early October, I was fearing a relapse, so I stayed in bed most of the time when I wasn't working. I used sick days as the cycles narrowed.

I received the final forms for my father's probate in the fall. Only one sheet contained any information, and it was such a mess, I could not concentrate well enough to sort it out. There was a Xeroxed check ledger that was difficult to read. Xeroxed bills seemed incomplete. The organ, one of my designated items, as well as the car, were listed on the probate.

Meanwhile, I became more afraid to drive. I wondered if I was losing peripheral vision. My short-term memory was failing. I was uncertain of my mental faculties in general.

I joined the ME/CFS support group and learned there had probably been no recovery but a remission. I learned that retroviruses penetrate one's DNA and alter it all while one's T-cells are destroyed. It would be years before learning where the retrovirus came from and how we acquired it.

One-third of ME/CFS patients have blood dyscrasias. Only five percent completely recover from ME/CFS and that takes three to five years. Sixty percent partially recover in five years, another ten percent partially recover in six years, and the rest slowly improve as much as they are going to over ten years. At least twenty-five percent are bedridden or homebound at some point in their illness or permanently. Some are vegetables due to the CNS inflammation. I did not know where I would fall, but I hoped for full recovery. I was three years into the disease.

A nutritionist had informed me that, if I had ME/CFS, I was gluten intolerant. Most doctors seemed totally unaware. I was grateful I had found a hematologist who had at least recognized the illness. Most other medical doctors were not even interested in learning more about the illness in order to treat it more intelligently. They even prescribed things that were contraindicated. Years later, when the CFIDS Association began sending out pamphlets to doctors to better inform them, my medical doctor told me he was too busy to read it! On my yearly visit for my physical, he insisted I should have a shingles shot.

"I shouldn't have anything with virus, no vaccinations," I replied.

"You are going to become more ill from shingles than you ever would otherwise."

I acquiesced. A week later, a rash developed on my face, and I became very viral and in bed four days a week. Over the next seventeen months the symptoms continued. My doctor was informed. Later, I heard about an ME/CFS patient who had blood dyscrasia, was treated but the treatment was wrong, and it pushed her into Hairy Cell Leukemia. My hematologist had not tried to treat us and had only recommended rest and a good diet. How lucky!

There were other problems for ME/CFS patients too. In addition to central nervous system symptoms that varied in type and severity with each patient, there was the problem with radiation if one had to have X-rays and CAT scans. My dentist insisted on X-raying my teeth and became angry if I refused. X-rays put me in bed for two days. When I broke my leg, there were X-rays monthly for six months then a downhill slide occurred which resulted in the usual, frequent flu-like symptoms. It took two years to fully recover. Lastly, on my annual eye check with my ophthalmologist, she informed me there was a higher incidence of glaucoma with ME/CFS patients. Despite all this, I felt blessed Vickie and I could, in a limited way, live half-decent lives compared to the stories from the CFIDS Association about those who were totally homebound. Later in 2015 I learned from the CFIDS Association the NIH allots only $2.50 per person for ME/CFS research. Lost productivity for this group and medical costs contribute to a total economic burden of up to 24 billion dollars annually.

TEN

RELAPSE

1990 - 1991

Julie called in late fall to tell me we were running out of money. I didn't understand. I thought we had enough for two years. When I asked where all the money had gone, Julie simply said, "For bills." I was sinking into the fog of illness again and couldn't sort it out.

"I can't afford this," I told her. "I don't want to pay. I want to sell the house!"

"It isn't a good time to sell. Jim can take over your part and when we sell you can pay him back from the sale."

"Couldn't we work something out?" I pleaded. "I don't use the house and you and your family do."

"You own half and are responsible for half the expenses and upkeep. Jim will help, don't worry," Julie soothed, side-stepping the main issue.

I felt unable to pursue this further, so

agreed that Jim could pay my portion of the expenses and I would pay him back when the house was sold, still thinking the sale of the house would be soon. *Why hadn't she been as helpful when the lakeshore property was an issue?*

*   *   *   *   *

The day arrived when I could not return to work, and I reluctantly handed in my resignation. How was I going to support myself and carry hospitalization? COBRA was still in effect, but money was in short supply. How could I get out of the obligation of the apartment?

My guardian angel must have been looking out for me. First, the money from my accident arrived, the full amount the insurance company would pay. Gabe's words came back to me and were prophetic. The detailed notes and papers I kept, my lawyer informed me, enabled him to present the best "soft tissue" case he had ever handled. Strangely Gabe had never appeared on the unit again, I only knew his first name. Gabriel who? God's angel? My lawyer informed me that after his fees and court costs I would receive nine thousand dollars. Four thousand went into my IRA and the rest would help me get by as I could no longer work. Secondly, the apartment management sent out notices that leases would no longer be renewed each October. All leases would be on the same schedule and thereafter would be renewed each March 1. Until then, rentals would be from month to month. What a break! This would allow me to give a thirty-day notice and be out of the building by mid-February of 1991.

The following March I applied for disability. By that time, I had lost my peripheral vision and the mental fog was even worse. I was flu-like, couldn't walk very far, had severe headaches, an aching body, gastrointestinal symptoms, photophobia and soap burned my skin. Over the next month I had to bathe only in water. My math skills had deteriorated drastically, and I was now unable to even remember how to balance my checkbook. I would lie quietly on my couch in the evening and listen to music as severe photophobia prevented me from doing much else. When able to watch television or look at a movie, I didn't always understand the action or the plots. For example, a friend brought over the movie, *Total Recall*, for us to watch but the point of the story totally escaped me. I never suspected for a moment that the problem lay with me.

I moved out of the apartment and went to live with Vickie. Social Security Disability called and quizzed me. My doctor suggested I was depressed and not relapsing. I replied hotly, "Yes, I'm depressed all right! Depressed I can't work and pay my bills!" Social Security called again to tell me they needed to hear from my physician, who had not been in touch. I prepared a history for my doctor and chronologically presented the symptoms that he had not bothered to take. My doctor submitted the needed information, and my application was approved. Disability payments would begin in October of 1991. I was relieved at the wonderful news. The amount was small and would barely cover my townhouse payment, but it was better than nothing. My hope of eventually returning to work had not dimmed.

Some of my furniture was put in storage and some taken to Brad's, where Vickie and I stayed. Brad took care of the moving bill and made sure there was money to cover my expenses if I came up short.

Vickie encouraged me to stay over the next few months. She wasn't feeling well due to an increase in the severity of her symptoms. Since she had given up her competitive skaters to other pros, her income had been substantially diminished. Despite that, she always managed to pay her father rent for use of his home. If there was any surplus in my budget each month, I tried to help her out.

Julie urged me to stay with her and Jim, but the thought made me uncomfortable. Vickie didn't want me to go, and she urged me to tell Julie. Then, my sister began urging me to come for Easter and sing in the choir, saying the choir really needed help. With supreme effort on both our parts, Vickie drove me to Williamsport. I managed to get the music ready but was so ill I sang the early service and immediately went to bed. Then I got up for the second service and was back in bed the rest of Easter.

After the second service, the choirmaster said I should have majored in music. I explained I had wanted to but had not been encouraged in that choice. Julie interrupted, sounding very annoyed. "She wanted to get married—that was more important! She could have gotten her degree in music after nursing."

I was stunned, more by Julie's tone than her words. In actuality my marriage occurred as soon as my education was finished; then I had embarked on working full time to put my husband through college. We wanted to start a family, so my pursuit of a music degree never materialized. Julie had always been understanding and sympathized with my frustration. This was the first time she had sounded totally disgusted and made it a blame game. I concluded Julie was just having a bad day.

While I was visiting, Julie and Jim asked about the car, and I told them that the motor was finished. They claimed the engine light had never flashed before when they had it. Later, Alison refuted that. I related that the mechanic had informed me there were iron filings in the oil and the motor was finished. Julie did not ask, and I did not tell her that Brad had replaced it. The Easter weekend over, Vickie and I returned home.

Julie kept calling and, when she could no longer be put off, I reluctantly made plans to return. The unease I felt continued. Despite the increased central nervous system inflammation, I was experiencing a slightly higher level of awareness. The thought of spending time with Julie disturbed me, but I felt obligated to respond to her persistent coaxing. My plan was to proceed with caution. *What was my intuition trying to tell me*? I was now in my fourth year of illness, and it was two years and six months since probate had ended.

* * * * *

The week before I left for Williamsport, Julie called and asked which bedroom I would like. I told her I preferred the larger one with the twin beds. If Julie needed the room for company, I would sleep in the smaller guest room, though it had a bed with an older, hard mattress. Julie said she would get the room ready. We agreed on weekly rent, the same as my last stay.

When I arrived, Julie carried my luggage to the small room with the double bed and deposited my things. "This bed really isn't very comfortable for me," I said, surprised.

"Oh, I probably misunderstood. Did you ask for the twin bed? The problem is that this room is clean, and the other isn't, so I guess you'll have to stay here for the time being." Julie finished in a charming, warm manner and kissed me on the cheek.

I silently scolded myself. My sister was concerned for me, wasn't she? "Okay," I relented. "I can give it a try, anyway."

During the first three days, things seemed to get off on the wrong foot. In a casual comment over coffee one morning after my arrival, I said in a wishful tone, "I wish we could have sold the lake property for more or been able to hold on to it until it was worth more. I sure could use the money right now." Julie's countenance tightened: she looked annoyed and didn't respond. Observing her reaction, I said no more.

On the second morning, I asked where to shop for Alison's birthday and for some suggestions on what to buy her. I hadn't been able to find petite sizes. Julie looked up from the morning paper she was reading and shot back irritably, "Vickie is so big! She is r-e-a-l-l-y big!"

Vickie was 5'9" and weighed 145 pounds since she had relapsed due to less activity. By eating all the time, she felt less viral. Prior to the relapse, she had been 130 pounds.

Julie was distant with me for several days and we barely spoke. I was walking on eggshells again. I was puzzled by Julie's behavior and finally had to ask Liz Alison's size and where to shop for her. Liz offered to do it for me.

My fibromyalgia symptoms worsened. The hematologist had advised rest. Tylenol sometimes took the edge off, but Julie thought the symptoms were from depression. I no longer cooked or baked as I had previously. I tried to relax by sitting in a comfortable chair, away from the busier parts of the house.

Something was amiss with Julie. Was it resentment? Had the first three days set the tone? Had my lack of activity around the house not been what Julie liked and expected? When asked, she denied there was any problem. To compensate, I made sure to set and clear the table and wipe up. I would help prepare the salad at dinner time. I was now in emotional as well as physical discomfort.

Julie's resentment persisted. I could no longer go shopping. I wasn't asked. Julie went alone or with Liz. Money was in short supply, and I had no energy anyway. One afternoon, Julie abruptly announced she wouldn't be home for dinner and that I would have to prepare a roast for Jim. She gave me directions for dinner and left. On another occasion, she came home after one of her weekly luncheons with the girls and was slurring and bleary-eyed. She directed me to get dinner for Jim and added emphatically, "I'm not hungry and I'm not going to cook!" I did as she directed despite the pain I was experiencing.

I reverted to my main enjoyment, reading, but had to read in short spurts due to the photophobia. At such times, I would put my head back on the chair, close my eyes, try to visualize, and go into silent meditation. One day, Alison sought me out. I was seated in my comfortable chair, with my head back and eyes closed. She seemed to sense my discomfort and confided to me that she believed my pain was caused from the mattress, that it was the worst one in the house. She suggested I ask to change beds. Encouraged by my niece's support, I asked Julie if I could move.

"No, you can't. David needs that bed for his nap when he is here!"

"Couldn't David take his nap in your bedroom?"

"No!" Julie snapped. "He doesn't like it there." That was the end of the discussion.

On another occasion, Julie told me I was using too much toilet paper and should only need four squares. "You shouldn't need as much as you are using for that little butt."

With my increased awareness, things around the house began to look familiar. I noticed an unusual Nippon egg warmer in Julie's glass cupboard. I remembered it had been designated to her. There were some whimsical dishes, some of which I was to receive in lieu of a creamer and sugar, which also sat in the cupboard. I tried desperately to think of a way to handle this delicate situation. It took a while, but I was finally able to get my thoughts together.

"I think there has been some kind of miscommunication," I said. "I am supposed to have half of the whimsical dishes."

"Take the ones you want."

"Do you have papers I can wrap them in as well as a small box?"

"No."

"What about these newspapers?" I motioned toward a stack on a small bench.

"Jim wouldn't want any newspapers touched." Julie made no more effort to be helpful. The Nippon whimsical pieces of my grandmother's were at least a hundred years old, and rather than risk having them break due to no protective packing, I left them.

On top of my sister's dresser, I also noticed a Victorian glass jar with roses engraved on its brass lid. It had been our maternal grandmother's and had sat on our mother's dresser until the year after Dad's death. I struggled to remember if it was a designated item. Propped behind the jar was an antique photograph of Dad and his brothers when he was ten years old. Once again, I was troubled by items being kept for "safe keeping". When I asked Julie about it, she claimed Dad had given these things to her. In my slowness, it didn't occur to me that the picture had not shown up until after Dad's death. I had forgotten that Dad had complained to me that Julie was taking things out of the house without his permission.

One day we were seated at the kitchen table, having just finished lunch. Julie pulled a silver piece from her purse with Dad's full name and address engraved on it, with her keys attached. She saw me looking at it curiously and said, "Oh, look what I found!" I said nothing but didn't like it.

One day I made a comment once more about dividing our family items. "There should be things we should be dividing. I don't understand why that hasn't been done. When do you think we could do that?"

"I don't know," Julie said, her head bowed. She walked away to the sink to get a glass of water before walking out of the room. Minutes later, she returned with a hand full of Indian jewelry that had belonged to Mom.

"You want to divide?" she snarled. "Well, you can divide THIS!" She firmly slammed the hand-full of jewelry down in the center of the kitchen table. "You know," she went on, "my girls should have their grandmother's things. After all, they *loved* their grandmother!"

The girls had not been named in the

will. She was implying that Vickie did not deserve anything, yet Aunt Beckie had given her silver pieces of our maternal grandmother's. I knew Vickie certainly didn't have the contacts with Mom and Dad that Julie's girls did, so the relationship wasn't as close. Still, I avoided conflict and instead asked if this was all we were going to divide.

Julie looked away. "There isn't anything much to divide." She said no more other than to tell me where she would put the Indian jewelry for me to sort through at my leisure. Mom had an 18K gold wedding band. I did ask if all jewelry wasn't going to be put on the table and dispersed. Julie never answered. Then I confirmed what we had agreed upon, that she'd be given two diamonds of the three available to the girls and I would receive one.

"That way, someday, each girl can have one," I reiterated. Julie then offered me the "Grandmother" ring Mother had loved and bought herself. The stones were genuine, but the ring was 10K gold with alloys. I didn't remember this until I saw it and agreed to take it. After all, it was Mom's, and I had nothing at this point.

Julie made nasty remarks not only to me but to Jim as well. One day, he inadvertently locked himself out of the house while working on the lawn. Julie went into a tirade, showing him with disgust how the lock worked and explaining in minute detail what had been done wrong: "You do this! Then you do this!" Jim quietly stood and watched her. I was appalled at how inappropriate my sister was acting and how Jim cowered. He just got quiet. At times, Julie came home after an afternoon of cards, lunch, and cocktails with the girls and berated him at the family coffee hour for a variety of things. He would quietly excuse himself and go downstairs to his small office, where he always had paperwork to command his attention. If he washed his hands in the half bath and didn't leave it exactly as he had found it, he was assailed and told to go to the basement and wash. Jim silently continued to wash his hands in the half bath. "He paid for the remodeling and therefore he thinks he can mess it up as much as he wants!" Julie snapped.

Julie had red potatoes for dinner as often as three nights in a week. I didn't know whether my sister wished me to leave or if she was trying to annoy Jim. The question was answered when he said, "Honey, we have had red potatoes three nights in a row."

"Well, they were on sale!" Julie shot

back.

I always tried to maintain some sense of serenity, but at one of the Friday afternoon coffee hours Julie erupted in an unusually nasty fashion. Alison had expressed to me how glad she was that I had exposed Alex to music. I told my niece that my mother and aunt always said that I could sing before I could talk.

Resentfully, Julie interrupted, "Where did you get THAT idea?"

"Aunt Beckie and Mother told me that story many times."

"Well, they were wrong!" my sister said angrily. "You couldn't sing until you were older."

One day during the usual coffee hour, Julie was reminiscing about her girls' performances in school. She spoke glowingly of her daughters before she turned to me and said, "You flunked the third grade, you know." I didn't recall ever being held back in school.

On another occasion, while discussing insurance and investments with Jim, he asked me when Dad had retired. "Two years after I graduated from nurses' training." Julie had walked into the room just as Jim asked the question. She exploded, "Where did you come up with that? He worked longer than that. He retired six years after you graduated! Where do you get these ideas?" She glared at me as if I were insane. Later when I was no longer with Julie and Jim, I found an old newspaper clipping among my memorabilia verifying my own recall. I wanted to send it to my sister but refrained. Why did she have to be so nasty?

Whenever Alison complained about Liz, Julie jumped to Liz's defense, sharply criticizing Alison for her comments. When Liz spoke negatively about Alison, Julie joined in! Together they would laugh at Alison in her absence. Also, they made negative remarks about Dan, Alison's husband. I feared that in time this behavior would extend to Alex. On these occasions, I left the room. Before she passed, our mother had tried to make Julie more aware of her negative attitude, but it had fallen on deaf ears.

In one of my frequent financial conversations with Jim, he told me the girls wanted to keep my parents' house. Shocked, I wondered why Julie hadn't told me. I was letting Jim pay my portion of the bills in my belief that the house would soon be sold, and Jim would be paid back from my share of the proceeds. Financially I was between a rock and a hard place.

In the year I had spent trying to get back to work, then relapsing, Aunt Beckie had begun falling in her home. Julie and Jim spent several weekends looking at long-term care facilities and chose the one they thought best. Fortunately, it was in Bay Harbor, an easy distance from our hometown. Julie complained to me about the responsibility. I told her to bill the estate if she thought she should be paid for her efforts, but I couldn't help think about Aunt Beckie, who had a housekeeper, Faith Lowery, whom my aunt paid but who had gone above and beyond to care for her. Another close friend had also done all she could and asked nothing for her extra time, "It is enough that Beckie is my friend and has been for years." Aunt Beckie had been a second mother to Julie but even more so to me. She had lived with us frequently throughout our lives due to difficult circumstances arising in her own life. My view was that anything done for the family was because they were family, period.

* * * * *

As usual, we all went to the homestead for July Fourth. Alison, the baby, and I left first and Jim and Julie were to follow that evening. Liz and her children would come later. Dan had stayed behind. That evening, Julie called to inform Alison they would not be able to leave until the next morning. Inadvertently, I walked into the room where she was seated with her back to the door and overheard her as she sobbed desperately. "Why do I have to be here alone with her? You promised!" Quietly, I backed out of the room.

That evening, after dinner, I told Alison of my possible plan to stay at my parents' house since I could no longer work. My plan included putting Mother's bed she had purchased when she had leukemia in the downstairs second bedroom. I said that I hoped it would not put anyone out. The downstairs second bedroom was next to the only bathroom in the house and convenient for my middle-of-the-night visits that had begun with the relapse. The bottoms of my feet, on arising for the nightly visits or on first arising in the morning, had become extremely painful. The long distance from the farthest small, back bedroom in which I had been sleeping since dad's death, was difficult for me to negotiate.

"Well, you can't use this room," Alison announced, indicating the second downstairs bedroom. "Mother says we need this room for our things."

There was a large closet in the room and the family did tend to use it as a catchall, but there was a room off the kitchen with a closet that could be used in the same way, as well as a summer kitchen where they could have put more of their things. Frankly, I didn't care if the room was crammed as long as the bed fit. Obviously, this issue had already been discussed in the family and the decision had been made to refuse my use of the second bedroom. It was just another stressful situation when all I wanted was to be comfortable.

Alison added, "You know, we all, including the little ones, will be coming and going. We use the house, and it will continue that way. That means we will be coming in on you whenever we want."

I felt Alison was acting inappropriately as this was Julie's and my home, but answered as graciously as possible, "Why, Alison, you sound as though you think that is a problem. It's not. You are welcome here anytime when I am here. You should know that."

When Julie, Jim, Liz, and Josh arrived, Alison must have reported the conversation to them, because Julie repeated to me what her daughter had said and Liz chimed in, "If you don't like where you are sleeping, go and stay at Aunt Beckie's."

"Her house is a mess, "I replied, "and I shouldn't have to go there to be comfortable. Also, there are no closets." I began to feel strongly that I needed to get away from this family for a smoother recovery. It seemed irrelevant to them that I was half owner of the house and paid half the bills. Not feeling able to take them on, silence was my rule.

Another incident that occurred shortly after their arrival was that Julie immediately asked Alison for the keys to the house. Alison had given them to me. When Julie learned this, she commanded, "I want the keys, NOW!" She extended her hand and obviously it had to happen immediately. What had happened to my sister? Did she really think I wouldn't give her keys back?

I retrieved the keys from my handbag and handed them to my sister. "Here they are," I said obligingly.

All during that Fourth of July stay, Julie made it clear a number of times that she and Jim would be constantly using the house for six or seven months of the year and would often be there if and when I was there. I assured my sister that would be fine, but it seemed to be a problem for her. Julie and I visited Aunt Beckie over that weekend, who at ninety-one played the piano for the other patients at the long-term care center. She seemed to be doing well but kept asking when she would be going home.

Besides the family silence whenever I entered the room, there were other incidents during that stay. One afternoon, Julie proposed we go to Aunt Beckie's house to check on it. I did not know that the housekeeper still had the key and frequently checked the house. When we arrived, Julie asked if I would mind if she took a cat cage of Aunt Beckie's for travel. I assured her it was alright. I noted a Jim Lee oil painting of Aunt Beckie's was missing, but Julie insisted there had been no painting on that wall. I knew she wasn't being truthful and wondered if she had taken it or given it away without my consent. Why couldn't she be forthcoming? As we walked through the living room on our way to the front door, we passed the huge Victorian black walnut mirror that stood there. With admiration in my voice, I commented, "Oh I saw a mirror like that in the foyer of the townhouse in Illinois. It was gold-leafed and just stunning!" It was only an observation and meant no more than that.

Julie put her face almost nose to nose with me and said in a threatening manner,"

If you want that mirror, you will have to deal with ME, FIRST!"

I was stunned and after a thoughtful pause I replied, "If you want the mirror, then I would like Mother's bedroom set."

Perhaps my tone of voice would come across as a suggestion rather than a demand. Julie did not answer. The moment passed and for the rest of the time Julie managed to be pleasant. Would there be more incidents like this? *There must be a fair way to divide things without these kinds of challenges. Why is she like this?* There were no answers forthcoming. Before the death of our parents, we had always been so close. I was seeing a side of Julie I didn't recognize.

* * * * *

Julie, Jim, and I returned to Williamsport as my pain and discomfort continued to plague me. Once again, I asked Julie if I could sleep in the twin bed in the other bedroom and tried to make clear to her why. Julie's response was the same. "No, David likes this room for his nap!"

A few days later, I found a small, inflated rubber raft—like the ones children use in a pool—on my bed. I heard Jim and Julie laughing downstairs in the kitchen. "She's grandstanding, you know.

She doesn't have pain," I heard Julie say.

I could not stay any longer! I had been invited for what reason I was no longer sure. My plan was to bide my time and tactfully figure a way out of this. Julie seemed totally oblivious to my health. My sister must have been threatened by my presence. This was a new revelation to me. My sister was a power player. The last things I needed were tension, intrigue, deceit, and power struggles. My priorities were first, physical comfort. Secondly, peace and serenity. A distant last was to be treated with fairness and honesty regarding the estates. The first two priorities were by far the most important as they would be to any ill person. There was rarely a thought about the third except when Julie made issues about cherished or household property or told me things that didn't feel *right*. Julie's lack of transparency with the probate only reinforced my determination to leave, recover as best I could, and try to get the estate settled the way it should have been in the first place.

ELEVEN

THE RESCUE

1991

One day, I was propped on pillows, sitting up in bed, when Liz entered. She sat on the edge of the bed and began to discuss information she had gleaned about my condition. She said I was very depressed.

"Psychologically or physiologically?" I asked. "There is a lot of central nervous system inflammation with this illness."

"Psychologically," she said. "I know a man who knows a lot about ME/CFS and there is a lot of depression."

"I don't feel I am any more depressed than any other chronically ill person. Unlike true depression, I want to do things but can't, whereas with depression, people don't want to do things and lose interest in life."

Liz continued insistently, "Well, he really knows what he is talking about, and he says your CFIDS Association information is old." She persisted with the man's credentials. Feeling irritated by Liz's insistence, I said no more and gracefully tried to change the subject.

A few weeks later, Vickie called and asked me to join her and her father as they planned to go to the hometown in early August for ten days. I was relieved to get away from my situation at Julie's. Vickie would pick me up on the way and Brad would arrive two or three days later or as soon as he could wrap things up at work.

My joy was short-lived when Julie, after being informed, said the family would be going to the hometown in a few days. I asked Julie for my key to the house. She answered off-handedly, "You don't need your own key. Just get it from the caretaker when you arrive."

"That is an impractical suggestion to awaken the caretaker if it is a late hour."

"Just let him know you are coming."

Emphasizing every word, I said, "Give me a key that will be mine!" Julie reluctantly handed me a set of keys to the house.

That evening, before I left, I said to Julie, "Let's divide the antique jewelry and give me what is designated to me."

"There is not that much," she answered.

"What about what I am to receive?"

"There is nothing in writing."

I was shocked. *Does that mean she keeps everything as Representative?*

Once again, Julie couldn't look at me. "There's just not that much," she repeated with finality in her voice.

When Vickie arrived, I happily climbed into the car and after comfortably propping myself with pillows we were off. It was a good trip. Vickie was talkative and cheerful. She did inform me that, when Aunt Julie and Uncle Jim arrived, she would not stay at the house but would join her father at the farm. Disappointment washed over me, but I tried not to show it. When we arrived and unloaded the car, our luggage was deposited in the downstairs bedroom so I could be comfortable in my mother's special bed and closer to the bathroom. Vickie said, "I don't think Aunt Julie will allow this."

"Aunt Julie won't care. She has always said first come, first served, and besides, she would want me to be comfortable." The fact Julie had refused me the comfortable bed at her home, as well as Alison's previous warnings, totally escaped me.

"Mother, don't you get it? Why do you think I don't stay here anymore?"

"I thought you liked the shower at the

farm."

"No! I just said that. I stay there because we are not wanted here. I saw it begin when Grandma died, then it really changed the minute Grandpa died. Your sister tries to run everything. It has to be her way or no way. The back bedroom is your place and that's where you are supposed to stay! She manipulated you out of your bedroom in the first place. Do you really think she is going to let you sleep anywhere else?"

"Let's see what she does," I replied calmly.

"She will kick you out!"

"No, she won't, and maybe Jim will even be a little more thoughtful. I will sleep here in my mother's bed, and we will see what they do."

Vickie shook her head in defeat. "Alright, but when she takes over, I'm leaving. If I'm wrong, I will stay with you after they arrive."

Before Julie and Jim arrived, I had three wonderful, ten-hour nights of sleep. Also, the nightly trips to the bathroom were easy. The evening they arrived, we had gone out to visit some friends as well as Aunt Beckie and, when we returned, Jim and Julie were sitting at the kitchen table, looking upset. Julie, once again, had a tense expression and Jim was actually pouting.

"What's wrong? You seem upset," I asked as I entered through the back door into the kitchen.

"Nothing," Julie answered coolly and looked away.

"Well, I'm tired. I'm going to bed. Goodnight."

Vickie silently followed me from the room. We entered the bedroom and I found Jim and Julie's luggage piled on both beds. Vickie stared at me meaningfully and raised her eyebrows as if to say 'I told you so..."

Returning to the kitchen, I said, "I can't go to bed with your luggage on the bed. What do you want me to do with it?"

There was a long silence before Julie said, "I *told* you where we sleep!"

"But you said it was first come, first served."

"I don't recall ever saying that! We will help you carry your luggage upstairs," Julie announced firmly.

Vickie raised her eyebrows once more. Julie and Jim purposefully arose from their chairs and proceeded to carry my luggage upstairs, but not before Vickie got hers and said goodbye.

Julie looked at me with a puzzled expression. I told her Brad was at the farm. "Julie," I added, "I have been sleeping in

Mother's bed because it is so much more comfortable for me."

"Well, Jim has a bad knee and can't climb the stairs."

Jim had no trouble climbing the stairs with my luggage, and there had been no problem with him negotiating the stairs in his home.

Over the next few days, I stayed in my room much of the time, reading and doing simple stretching exercises as every muscle in my body ached. When Alison and Dan arrived, I confided, "I wanted to be more comfortable. I didn't want to put anyone out."

"I suppose Dad pouted," Alison replied.

"As a matter of fact, he did."

"I think that's what upsets Mother. She doesn't mean to be thoughtless."

The matter was dropped.

That weekend, after the girls and their families left, I said to Julie, "I'd like to try the bed in my old room."

"Well, go ahead," she snapped, "but in the first place that's not your room. In the second place, Liz and Josh need that room because they have David." The message was, 'Don't plan to stay there."

"I don't want to put them out. I'm just trying to find a comfortable bed. But why do you say it isn't my room?"

"Because I slept there too. It wasn't your room any more than mine!"

"Which was my room, then?"

"You slept wherever there was space for you!" Julie snapped.

In truth, Julie had slept in the second bedroom for two years with me before she left for college. I slept there for six years more before leaving for college, and Julie returned for a year before she was married and used the room but slept in the front guest bedroom when I came home for visits from college. Brad and I used the second bedroom for seventeen years. Mom had gotten a cot for Vickie and that is what David now occupied.

I tried the bed in my old bedroom that night, but I was still uncomfortable. My mother's bed was best for my condition. I told Julie, hoping she would come to the conclusion that Mom's bed should be moved into the second downstairs bedroom out of kindness. As usual, she ignored me.

Later that week, while seated in a comfortable chair reading, I looked at my mother's China cabinet, which was situated across the room from me. On the wall, next to the cabinet, were Mother and Grandmother's beautiful Victorian, hand-painted plates from Germany and Austria, along with a large plate I had given my mother one year for Christmas. Also, there was my grandmother's aqua plate with white roses, much sought after Prussian, the most beautiful and most valuable of the collection. The smaller plates that had graced the China cabinet were gone but, according to Julie, put away for safe keeping.

Just then, my sister entered the room. She pointed to the large aqua plate and hissed, "I'm taking this plate! You can have this one!" She pointed to the Lenox Limited Edition plate of Monet's 'Garden at Giverny' I had given my mother. Julie was twisting the agreement but, once again, I didn't want to fight over a plate. I wanted to avoid conflict. My sister marched out of the room with the coveted plate.

I felt as if I would burst. When no one was around, I called Brad and pleaded with him to take me to dinner. I had to get away. He promised to pick me up in two hours, at five that afternoon. *What a relief!*

With feigned politeness, I waved goodbye to Jim and Julie, as did Brad and Vickie from the car as we pulled away. As soon as we were around the corner, I burst into tears. Brad and Vickie began to laugh.

My anger flared. "Why are you laughing at me? What is so funny?"

"We're not laughing at you. We are laughing with relief. You have finally realized something is wrong," Brad said.

Vickie added, "What have I been trying to tell you since Grandma died?"

Without answering her question, I said, "I can't stay with them anymore. They don't want me around, and I certainly don't want to be where I'm not wanted—and I can't live alone." I proceeded to tell them of all the incidents with my sister and her family.

"We'll figure something out," Brad said when I had finished.

"They act as though they own the place! I haven't been able to pay for the last eight months. Julie assured me the house would soon be sold and I could pay her back, then I find out from Jim they are going to keep it! Julie never told me!"

"Pay them now, for God sakes!" Brad said, his voice filled with urgency. "I'll give you the money! What have you gotten from your father's estate besides the money?"

"Nothing except my half of what she identified as a small insurance policy. I never saw any paperwork, so the total amount is unknown to me."

Brad frowned as he gripped the steering wheel. "Have you received an accounting of the money?"

"Some very confusing stuff."

"Have you divided the household items you mentioned she was protecting?"

"No."

"Why not?"

"I don't know," I replied. "She seems reluctant when I ask, and I don't feel well enough or alert enough to push it. My instincts tell me I would come out badly if I did."

Brad shook his head. "Those items should not have been removed to protect them. They are joint property. They are supposed to have been divided by the end of Probate. She is a manipulator. She is not acting the way a Representative should. Don't keep hoping she's going to divide. She isn't!"

I sobbed. "I have always thought she would bring the items back. I could never do that to her."

"She won't bring them back!" Brad replied with impatience. "She will only bring back what she doesn't want!"

Tears welled in my eyes. "What can I do?"

"I don't know. We will bide our time and just see what she does," Brad said. "You will go back and act as you have in the past. We'll work something out."

Even though my ex couldn't come up with anything concrete at the moment, his reassuring words made me feel much better.

"Oh, Mom!" Vickie said. "I'm so relieved you finally see what I have been talking about." She rubbed my shoulders affectionately from the back seat.

"I'm too sick to deal with this," I said. "Why can't Julie be kind, fair, and honest?"

"Because she is too selfish," Vickie replied.

"I just want to get along and it seems everything I say or do is taken the wrong way. Am I so terrible? Am I so out of it?"

Brad maneuvered his car through the light traffic. "You're not yourself, not as alert, but you're not that bad. Julie could be more understanding and caring. She wants you financially out of the way."

We arrived at a lovely restaurant Brad had chosen and ate dinner, our painful, earlier conversation put away for now. When we finished, Vickie assisted me into my sweater and hugged me, something she had not done in a while.

I squeezed her hand. "I am so sorry," I said. "You have been so right all this time and I have been so wrong."

* * * * *

There were not any firm plans as to when I would leave Jim and Julie's, but we decided I would spend time between Brad's and Vickie's. One of Vickie's bedrooms had been rented to a girlfriend temporarily to help Vickie with her expenses. I was not enthusiastic about living with two young girls, but I would stay wherever I could. Anything was better than what I was going through at Julie's. Brad and Vickie both kissed me on the cheek and deposited me back at the house. I walked into the house feeling refreshed and comforted.

I told Julie and Jim the next morning that I would leave over Labor Day and Brad would be picking me up. Julie seemed pleased, then informed me that Aunt Doris had invited me to stay for a week just before Labor Day. After the holiday, she and Jim planned to go on vacation. She wondered if I would housesit until they returned, and I agreed.

Julie and Aunt Doris had always been close, and I couldn't help but wonder if Julie had complained about me and Aunt Doris had volunteered to take me off her hands. Aunt Doris was only fourteen years older than my sister, and Julie looked more like Aunt Doris than her own children. They both liked to socialize and party and seemed to click with each other.

The week before Aunt Doris was to pick me up, Julie seemed in good spirits. One afternoon, she came into my room and sat on the edge of the bed. She had an inexpensive chain in her hand that—looked to be in poor condition.

"There isn't much for jewelry in either estate, but you want to divide things. Here is a chain of Mother's. I thought you might like it." Julie carefully handed it to me, as if it were some delicate, valuable piece.

The piece was so shoddy, I couldn't imagine my mother ever wearing it. Once again, to avoid conflict, I accepted the necklace. Then, Julie produced two jewelry boxes, one silver and one embroidered with small roses that played "Edelweiss" when the top was opened.

"Look through these," she said, "and see what you want. Mother only had costume jewelry." Once again, I had an uneasy feeling but chastised myself for my growing distrust.

"I gave Mother the embroidered jewelry box, so I will take that." Resentment boiled inside me. Julie still kept these things in her home four years after Dad's death. What would have happened if I hadn't started pushing her? I might never have seen the jewelry box or thought of it unless my memory had fully returned.

"Yes, I know you did. She loved that jewelry box and took it everywhere with her," Julie volunteered.

If she knew I had given Mother the jewelry box, why did she keep it for four years? Unwilling to confront her in her home despite her lies and deceit, I held my tongue and merely said, "I will look through the boxes later."

*   *   *   *   *

Aunt Doris arrived to take me to her home for a week. I was eager to go, relieved to be out of Julie's home, even if it was only for a week. When I returned, they would immediately leave on vacation and, when they came back, I would be off to Brad's. I knew I could last that long.

The long trip to Aunt Doris's wore me out. I was in bed for several days with my usual flu symptoms. Aunt Doris was solicitous and thoughtful. The bed she offered me was wonderful. When I began to feel better, she took me for rides wherever she had errands. Widowed, with four children, she was low-key and fun. I felt closest to my cousin Kerry, who was six years younger, had a great sense of humor and was full of energy and spirit. Kerry stopped by often and sometimes stayed overnight. Drew, Aunt Doris' son, and his wife invited us to dinner one evening. I found myself relaxing and enjoying the total change in atmosphere. They were all so fun-loving and humorous. Over dinner they would kid each other good-naturedly and tell funny stories. One evening, Aunt Doris took everyone out to dinner. I felt renewed and revived, thinking I could face the return to Julie's with more enthusiasm.

Aunt Doris and I spent quiet afternoons talking before I would lie down for my afternoon nap. On one of these occasions, she asked about some people from the hometown who were deceased. She had heard their children were involved in a serious family episode. I answered as to what I knew of the situation through Brad's brother, who had been in contact with one of the sons. When I finished, Aunt Doris replied, "Now, isn't that something? That is *exactly* the story I heard from Julie after she spoke with the son. You seem very accurate in your statements, not at all confused or wrong."

I was dumbstruck, unable to imagine or follow Julie's machinations. What was my sister saying about me? How many others had she told? Aunt Doris asked three times during my stay how I liked my nieces, and each time I answered that I liked them very much, that they were very nice girls. Aunt Doris also inquired about Alison, asking if Julie was still treating her shabbily while everything was 'Liz, Liz, Liz'. She added that my mother had always been upset about this. I answered that the situation seemed about the same. Though it appeared my mother had confided this to Aunt Doris, I didn't feel comfortable sharing.

Near the end of our time together, Aunt Doris confided that, when Dad had stayed with her for three weeks after Mom died, he complained that Julie was removing items from the house. She added he had seemed very upset. She asked me if I was aware of such occurrences and, if so, what would Julie have taken? I recalled the conversation with my father. I was a little surprised and puzzled as to why Aunt Doris was probing me about Julie, her favorite niece. I was uncomfortable with the way Julie was conducting herself as Representative, but I was uncomfortable as well in discussing this with Aunt Doris. When the time came for my visit to end, I reluctantly returned to Julie's, determined to enjoy the weekend as much as possible before she and Jim left on their trip.

The day after my return, Julie was talking to a neighbor, whom I knew fairly well, in the driveway. When I walked outside to say "Hello", both of them stopped talking and stared silently at me as I approached. *I'll be so glad to leave here,* I thought to myself. Is Julie telling others how out of it I supposedly am, like she had told Aunt Doris? I decided I would keep a diary so I could record all the negative behavior. Maybe a well person might not react as I was, and I wanted as accurate an account of my sister's deeds as possible.

Later the same day, Julie entered my bedroom and removed a ring from her finger. She said Mother had directed her to give it to me, plus a necklace which she brought out. Although I could not recall it at the time, my mother had instructed Julie before her death—and in front of me — to give me the ring Julie had been wearing for several years now. Mother had given Julie the best of the Indian jewelry with the comment, "You have what you want, now give that ring to Josie." Julie had cooperated and smilingly removed the ring from her finger and handed it to me. This second ring and necklace came as a pleasant surprise, and I treasured these pieces because our Mother had worn them often and wanted me to have them. I didn't care that they weren't my mother's best pieces. Julie showed me Mother's most beautiful pieces and said she wanted me to see what she had, so there would be no misunderstandings. She explained Mother had given them to her. It didn't occur to me to question why it had taken four years since Dad's death for Julie to give me the items. Julie also presented Mother's Waltham watch ensconced in a costume jewelry pendant mesh piece to me with, "Since Grandma's pendant watch can't be found, take this." Devastated I began to cry. Julie stood by silently with an unsympathetic look on her face. I realized my sister had ice water in her veins.

* * * * *

Jim and Julie left the following Tuesday morning for a trip east to the New England states. They would be gone for two weeks. Over the next week, I began to pack and ready myself for the trip to Brad's. Remembering Julie's invitation to look through Mom's two jewelry boxes, I sorted out the jewelry I could remember giving my mother as gifts and placed them in the embroidered jewelry box. The remaining pieces I planned to place in Mother's silver jewelry box.

When I opened the silver box, lined with red velvet, I noted there were small costume jewelry pieces and clumps of straight pins, safety pins, some rubber bands, and my maternal grandfather's driver's license at the bottom of the box.

In removing the junk, I noticed a chain. As I untangled the mess, I recognized it as a necklace Mom had worn as a girl—a wax seal necklace with a cameo. I remembered Julie had worn it right after Dad died. What I couldn't remember was that Mom had told me Julie wanted it and was to have it. When Julie had seen me staring at it, she never wore it again.

Julie loved jewelry too much and was too precise not to know where this piece was. I could only conclude she had put it in the box with the other odd things. Why had she chosen to do this, and what else was she plotting if she was willing to part with this piece? Up to now, she had only offered me junk. She may have placed the necklace there, hoping I would ignore the mess or, in my usual open style, show her what I had found, and in turn she would have said, "Oh, there it is! I don't have anything of Mother's." Or in her commanding way say, "Oh, there it is! I'm going to keep this," and quickly grab it out of my hands. I decided that, when my sister returned, I would make sure to wear it and see what she had to say. I placed the chain in my jewelry box under several other pieces. If she wanted this, she would have to trade something of better quality in return. She had other, more valuable pieces and that was why she was willing to risk losing this necklace. She hadn't done anything, so far, out of the goodness of her heart. My sister could no longer be trusted. I couldn't keep up with her devious games and plots. Her way of thinking was foreign to me.

Even with this discovery, I still couldn't pull all the pieces together. Julie intended to keep the pendant watch, which had been designated to me, telling me there was nothing in writing. She never mentioned our maternal grandfather's diamond ring. Why did there have to be all this intrigue when I was trying to get well? It would be a long time before I eventually remembered and began to wonder when Julie had checked the safe deposit box at the bank as directed by me the year before. It hadn't yet occurred to me that, on the next hometown visit, I should go to the bank and ask for their records.

I sorted through the Native American jewelry next. I decided to call my nieces and divide the pieces. Liz arrived first. "These were your grandmother's," I said. "Choose the ring and bracelet you would like."

"What about Vickie?" Liz asked.

"She likes it all, so it doesn't matter to her what she gets."

Liz chose her two pieces and asked why I was letting them do this. "Your grandmother has been dead seven years and Grandpa four, and it is way past time to divide. These matters should have been taken care of long ago." Liz looked through the other jewelry and said, "You gave this bracelet to Grandma, didn't you?"

I thought the gold bracelet was familiar. "Yes, I did, and I will take that with me." I did not comment on why Julie had kept my gift to Mother in her home this long after the probate. I asked Liz about a gold locket in the jewelry box and she said it had been her gift to her grandmother. "We should be able to take the things we gave, so take it."

Liz shook her head no. "I have no right to take what I gave Grandma without my mother's permission."

After Alison chose her set, a few old, odd pieces remained as well as a nice set for Vickie. I kept the old pieces, not for their beauty but for sentimentality. They were pieces Mom had bought on our trip together out west.

I began to suspect that the missing and protected items were all somewhere in Julie's house. I considered ransacking the place while she was out of town, but what then? Place all the items on her dining room table and confront her when she arrived home? I simply wasn't up to it. I would have to find a way to deal with the situation in a different and ethical manner if my sister wasn't going to fairly share and divide our inheritance. I reminded myself that Brad had assured me it wasn't going to happen. He was probably right.

TWELVE

A SLOW AWAKENING

1991

When Julie and Jim returned, there was the usual excitement in relating the details of their trip, then Julie brought out a small statue she had bought me as a thank-you for house sitting.

Later that day, Julie entered my bedroom and picked up Mom's silver jewelry box. "Did you find anything you wanted?" Unable to tolerate conflict, I told her that I hadn't found anything I really wanted. In truth, all that I wanted was what was designated to me, even though I was sometimes unable to recall what all that might be. I informed her that the girls chose the Indian jewelry they wanted, and I took the oldest of the pieces that were left. I was wearing the wax seal necklace, but Julie didn't seem to notice.

She smiled with satisfaction as she dropped a man's ring in my lap. "Here, this is for you."

I recognized it as my father's masonic ring he had worn when I was a little girl. The ring was bent out of shape, but I could have that fixed by a jeweler. The black onyx stone with the masonic insignia was intact. It was just another piece of shabby jewelry that Julie was trying to pawn off on me. In truth, Mom had designated it to me so I would have something of Dad's which I was unable to remember.

Then, Julie commanded, "Give me Mother's jewelry box!" She meant the embroidered music jewelry box I had given to Mom.

I went to the closet, picked it up, and handed it to Julie with, "This is mine, you know." Julie opened the box but, when I told her what I thought, she immediately closed the top and handed it back to me without going through the contents.

That evening, when I went to the kitchen to help with dinner preparation, Julie appeared extremely upset. "Do you have the keys?" She sounded accusatory. She meant the keys to our parents' home. I shrugged and shook my head. I had my own set now.

Julie went to a drawer in the kitchen and pulled out a small plastic bag. "They should be here," she said tersely, "but they're gone!" She began banging the drawers as she opened and closed them. "Are you sure?" Again, I perceived her question as accusatory, and answered firmly that yes, I was sure. I sat down at the kitchen table to observe this extreme upset over keys.

Finally, Julie marched to the telephone and called Liz. "Do you have the keys?" She sounded desperate. *What is wrong with her?* Did Julie think I had stolen her set of keys? Liz must have said "yes", because Julie visibly relaxed, drew a deep sigh and said, "Oh, good!" Then, "Oh no, it is alright that *you* have the keys." Disgust overwhelmed me.

The following day, Brad arrived and packed the car with all my belongings. Jim and Julie cordially invited him to stay for dinner, but he declined, saying we had a long drive ahead. Brad was aware how anxious I was to leave and didn't want to stay one second longer than necessary. I kissed my sister and brother-in-law goodbye and thanked them for their kind hospitality, telling them I would be back later for my two chairs. Julie shot back, "Possession is nine tenths of the law."

"Not to ethical people," I replied dryly.

Even as my awareness was growing, I had absolutely no clue as to the depth of

Julie's manipulations. I put my head back and slept for the better part of the trip.

As the miles distanced me from my sister, I began to relax and feel safe, sure deep within myself that I would get well now that my surroundings weren't suffused with intrigue and tension. I no longer recognized Julie. What one saw was an aristocratic, attractive, intelligent, warm, honest, and sincere person who was seductively and deceptively charming. Underneath she was really a person who was superficial, materialistic, and a master of deception and manipulation.

I had been at Brad's about a week when I received a call from Alison. "How are you feeling and getting along in your new surroundings?" she asked.

"The place is small, with two bedrooms, and easy to do the few things I am able to do every day without having to expend much energy."

"Mother was angry about you dividing the Indian jewelry. She says you should have done it when she was there."

"Funny, she didn't say anything when she wanted to see what I took." I did not reveal Julie's intrusiveness during that encounter. "It's time, Alison, for division. Grandma has been gone for seven years and Grandpa for four. Things should have been divided by now. This should have been taken care of much sooner." After we hung up, something occurred to me: Was that why Julie had wanted me to keep Dad during the summer, so she could pilfer through the house without interference?

Brad and I settled into a routine. He did the grocery shopping and I cooked, did the laundry and slowly, as my condition began to improve, started to do housework, breaking it down into small chores that could be easily managed. Brad wouldn't let me pay room and board. "You may never be able to work again," he said. "You'd better save what you have." When I was physically in pain, he quietly massaged my neck or shoulders. I couldn't have had a better caretaker. My bed was comfortable, and I could sleep through the night.

Brad had an outgoing personality, but he was also a homebody, content with watching sports and current events on the television. That had been difficult when we were married. I had wanted to join a dinner-dance group, but he declined. I wanted to go out to dinner occasionally and take a vacation once in a while, but vacations were spent hunting. Through the years, he never changed. We never did anything together except if his place of work had an event.

I was surprised when one day he suggested going out to dinner. Maybe being single all these years had caused him to make some changes in his life. Enthusiastically, I accepted his invitation, and we met another couple he knew. The restaurant was a small, charming room furnished in Early American and the food was wonderful, the company stimulating, and the evening enjoyable.

Three weeks after my departure from my sister's, I received a note from her in which she stated, "I failed to recognize how uncomfortable you were during your stay with us, probably because we have such a free rein at the house and we consider it ours, therefore, we didn't give a thought to anyone's possible discomfort." I was touched and pleasantly surprised by Julie's concern and her attempt to explain her behavior. I wrote back what I thought was a heartfelt note, with Brad's help.

About a week later, I received a call from Alison. "Aunt Josie, my mother is furious at your note. I can't figure out why. I think she is trying to find something to be angry at you about. I don't want to see your relationship destroyed, and when Mother becomes closed, there will never be a chance for reconciliation. She is always right, she is never wrong, and she never apologizes. Let me dictate a letter to her from you. She just seems very resentful."

In despair and with no understanding of what was taking place, I consented. Why was she acting like this? I didn't understand.

A week later, Alison called again. She was upset because her mother had taken offense to the latest note. "Her resentment is so severe—I think it has to come from early childhood."

Brad was out of town on police business, and I was alone. What were Julie's real issues? When Brad returned, he defined it for me. "Don't you understand what Julie is trying to do? She doesn't want you involved in anything about the house or what you are to inherit, and I'm convinced she doesn't want you to have anything at all. She will do anything she can to muddy the waters."

At Brad's urging, I called Julie and explained I would like an accounting of the expenses at the house. "I want to start paying again."

Sounding annoyed, Julie probed, "Why have you decided to start paying again?"

"Because I began receiving disability checks."

"You didn't want to pay the bills anymore!" she replied angrily.

"Because I couldn't pay the bills," I answered.

"You didn't WANT to pay!" Julie spat.

"I didn't want to pay because I *couldn't* pay!

"YOU DIDN'T WANT TO PAY!" Julie yelled.

I took a deep breath and calmly replied, "Whether you like it or not, I am half owner of the house—we are partners."

Julie seemed unable to stop her tirade. "YOU DIDN'T WANT TO PAY!" During a prolonged silence moments later, I hoped my lack of a response would calm her. Knowing Julie, she was probably flushed with triumph at getting the last word. She finally said that she would send the bills.

Brad asked for the final accounting of the indecipherable probate Julie had given me. He couldn't figure it out either. Julie's accounting made no sense to him. The probate records were incomplete and looked a mess, handwritten in illegible cursive.

I recalled Jim and Julie had taken an attorney friend and his wife to dinner. Perhaps that was the payoff and Julie kept the rest? She was not about to explain any expenditures she didn't wish to, so I would never really know for sure. However, at Brad's urging, I decided to try.

I called Julie and asked for records that were more forthcoming as "Brad and I couldn't figure it out." This elicited a furious explosion from my sister.

"Technically, everything is mine and my father's and I don't have to tell you anything! You were given my report and that's all you are going to get. You grandstanded at the house with the bed episode, and I am fed up with you!"

When Brad heard Julie's response, he said, "She is way out of line. Heirs are to be kept fully informed. However, if she had Power of Attorney, that is a different matter."

"She was given Power of Attorney after Mother died."

"Then be careful. You would have to go to court to get any more information unless there was a will." Julie probably surmised correctly that I was not aware of that. Information was power to my sister, and she seemed pathologically obstinate. She wasn't about to give up power. Brad called a friend who was a probate attorney and asked him to look at the house accountings.

Later he responded with, "It's the worst mess I have ever seen. My best determination is that there is $6,000 unaccounted for." He went on to explain, "A

Power of Attorney is a document whereby a person grants certain powers to another person.

Unfortunately, too often joint ownership is used as a means of giving another person access to funds rather than relying upon a Power of Attorney. Banks are notorious for suggesting joint ownership because it's easier for them. The problem is that the surviving joint owner frequently refuses to share the funds remaining after the first death, even though the deceased may have intended that the funds be shared. Assets change and therefore an inventory prepared when a will is made will soon be obsolete. The greatest safeguard is to retain ownership of all assets in one's sole name and rely upon the will to govern the distribution of assets after death."

I knew my father never meant to have Julie as a partner to all his assets and she had taken advantage of that—and there was a will. Julie had Power of Attorney only.

Brad explained further, "The Representative is to make sure that all heirs have a key if the premises is kept. You should have been given a key at the end of probate." Then, he related a story about his own family: "My name was on my mother's checking account with her. Upon her death, I relinquished it to the Representative. He called us for a meeting, where keys to the premises were dispersed and an accounting of all finances given as well. If there are any verbal wishes of the deceased, any reputable member of the family who is Representative will carry out their wishes. It doesn't have to be in writing. Your Mother and Dad sat us down together and made it very clear what we were to be given. Julie is carrying out her own wishes, not fulfilling the wishes of the deceased. As far as the use of the house goes, everyone informs the Representative, and the Representative informs his siblings when each plan to use the house. Once again, your situation is bizarre. There is a probate procedure and protocol, and Julie is totally disregarding it."

"Where can we get a copy of this?" I asked.

"At the County Probate Court Office."

Brad's friend sent us a final accounting filed with the Probate Court that Julie hadn't bothered to give me.

I refused to call Julie, so Brad made arrangements with her about using the house in late October as he planned to go to the family farm with his three brothers and their sons for hunting. He thought I would be more comfortable at my parents' house as the farmhouse was primitive, though the guys didn't mind roughing it.

When we arrived, I was able to sleep in my mother's bed. While Brad spent time at the farm, I read as much as the photophobia would let me, listened to my mother's records, played the organ, and visited Aunt Beckie, who was in the long-term care facility only eight miles away in Bay Harbor. I spent as much time with her as I was physically able.

I reminded Brad of Julie's demands for maintenance when using the house. The living room drapery rod wasn't working and hadn't been for three years. It wouldn't close. Brad fixed it. The summer kitchen was leaking rainwater in the corner where Mom's China cabinet sat. The cabinet's damage gave me the impression there had been leaking for quite some time. Brad and I carefully rolled the cabinet into a dry spot. Fortunately, it was an easy task as the cabinet had wheels so the glassware was not disturbed by the move. The third problem we noted was the back, inside kitchen door where one entered the kitchen from a utility area. Brad said that the door was sticking badly because no one had gone under the kitchen and jacked up the floor. He did that. He said, "Your father was very good about that, but the door is so difficult to open, I believe it hasn't been done since before he died."

After spending a week at the house, Brad and I prepared to leave. As we packed the phone kept ringing, and when I or he answered, no one was there. Brad guessed it was kids playing games.

Near the time we were to leave, Bob, a former student of Dad's from years ago, came over to exchange greetings and make sure the house was properly shut down. Bob wasn't really a maintenance man but had done this ever since Mom died as a favor to Dad. He was warm, personable, and seemed to particularly like Brad. They talked and laughed for a while and then Brad finished packing the car and we departed for Illinois.

Several days later, Faith Lowery, Aunt Beckie's caretaker, called and sounded upset. She and Bob both had keys to the house and watched over things. "Bob came over all upset. Apparently fifteen minutes after you left, Jim and Julie arrived and started going through closets and cupboards. He thought it was so odd, so he told me. Why would they act like that?"

I realized that was probably why the phone kept ringing. They were trying to determine if Brad and I had left. "They must think we are stealing things out of the house," I told her.

"Why would they think that?"

"Because people tend to judge others by their own behavior. Why do you think I have trusted her implicitly for so long?"

Faith, who had always been neutral, was silent for a moment. "I'm sure you like nice things," she said finally, "and would want to take them from the house."

"I love beautiful things, but I would never remove joint property from the house to have them. I couldn't live with myself if I did that to my sister, or even my worst enemy."

In November, Julie wrote a letter with the accounting of what I owed at the family home. Better a letter than a screaming phone call. I had begun to believe that Julie was alone when she acted out of line with me, and her family probably had no idea about the outrageous behavior. Her letter stated, "This is a factual accounting, a reminder of the circumstances following Dad's death, you're wanting to sell the house, prompting us to have to make our own financial decision which led to our assuming total responsibility for the house. This summer, you have shown little interest in regard to the house or its maintenance."

I was struck by Julie's position. What planet was she living on? I had told her I wasn't feeling well, but it seemed she preferred to ignore that as it probably didn't fit her plan. I thought she was aware of all the reasons I couldn't participate at the house, or even use it very much. The fact was, Julie, Jim, and their girls and families used the house all the time while Dad's money paid the bills before end of probate. Also, they were the ones who dragged their feet about selling the house or offering a decent price to me if they wanted to buy it. They knew, financially, I needed it sold. Why couldn't they appreciate the good deal they had up to now? I paid half the expenses until recently and lived several states away. Brad was right. Julie wanted the house for the maintenance I had been unable to pay.

Julie continued with another gem, "Before Jim began to pay all the expenses at the house after probate, the house ran on money from the estate that equaled the Blue Book value of the car." She was now telling me that I had to pay for the car and now owed money to run the house. No wonder the house money was gone in six months! I burst into tears.

I didn't answer Julie's letter right away as I had to slowly get my thoughts together.

After about a month, Julie called to inquire about my condition. I was having severe exacerbation and left my bed to answer the phone. I noticed the call was in the afternoon, when her family wasn't around. Disgusted by her phony demeanor, I told her I was "about the same." She then asked if I had received her letter.

"Yes. How unethical of you!"

"You have to pay for the car, you know, because it was in the probate." Unable to recall that I had told her that if I had to pay for the car, I didn't want it, I burst into tears and abruptly hung up. Julie, whenever the subject arose, continued to insist Dad had promised she would be compensated for the car. I was unable to reason as to why Dad would promise compensation for the car when Mom and Dad knew she had been stealing out of the house.

After much thought, my alleged lack of interest was rebutted in my return letter, six weeks later: *"This implies I have been disinterested. Since before Dad died, I have had nothing but disasters in my life—two major floods with water to the ceiling and FEMA declared our area a federal disaster. Then cleanup so filthy, I got ringworm and losses totaling $25,000 with no flood insurance, two surgeries, which helped lower my immune system along with the stress* *of the two floods, back problems with physiotherapy, staggering doctor bills above insurance payout for three years in a row, decimating my savings, then diagnosed with ME/CFS. I struggled to recover from flood damage and ready my house for rent. I knew something was wrong before diagnosis and knew I couldn't continue to work much longer. The disease reached its' crisis approximately one and one-half years after onset. I was so sick I couldn't think straight. Then was told I was pre-leukemic. As a result of the illness, I had major problems with work which eventually culminated in my medical termination... so you are absolutely right, I showed no interest in our home or in its' maintenance. I mistakenly have held the belief that all this time you understood. I should have known you didn't when I made an emergency trip with Dad to our agreed upon meeting point, my basement was filling with water, we had to be taken out in a boat, I told you it was an emergency situation and to hurry as I had to get back. We got to our destination and waited... and waited. We waited for over two hours because you had to get the oil changed!!"* Why hadn't they been as diligent about changing the oil in Dad's car, was my silent thought. "You have virtually unrestricted use of a lovely summer home." One of three, in Florida, our hometown, and

Williamsport but I didn't say it. "I feel you should be responsible for the maintenance. I would help if I were well and when I am there. The fact is I am rarely there, some five weeks in the last four years."

I did something I had never done to anyone before. I attacked her personally. *"I feel I am being beaten up in a sneak attack by your very indirect, subtle, veiled hostility. You act like a bully. You act like the oldest or only child who tends to see issues from the perspective of power and control and tries to jockey for the dominate position in relationships. You push and pull at your family to gain the dominant position and now you are doing it with me. I felt there were terms under which I could and could not come into the house, what I could and could not do, where I could and could not sleep. I could not have treated you that way. If the situation had been reversed, I would have treated you with love, respect and consideration. You would have come first with me. I would have given you choices that you deserve as my partner. I was in pain, had financially contributed my half until just recently and have rarely been around to interfere with your family summers in the hometown. You love your daughters, I love my daughter, but I have loved you longer. You are my sister, my partner and we have been best friends for 30 years. I was hurt this summer by your actions and that hurt persists. How sad that your positions on so many issues between us are so meanspirited."*

Julie wrote back and acknowledged that I was unable to help with maintenance due to illness, but added, "I cannot excuse you from maintenance duties even though you are rarely there. You own the house. You should help. The year before you became ill, you had shirked your responsibilities and didn't help in the yard for the week you spent there on the Fourth."

I was shocked at such pettiness.

Not willing to give up, Julie continued, "You have made serious accusations about me and my family. You have crossed the fine line of respect."

I attributed that remark to the charge that Julie's conduct was in question, and I had challenged her by pointing out that, "Oldest children often jockey for position." Both Julie and Jim were oldest children, but Jim didn't seem to do this sort of thing, at least in front of me. I had seen her try to jockey for position with Jim and her girls, and she always seemed to succeed. Her letter continued, "Did you think, according to the will and the final Voucher of Probate that you should receive half of the household contents, half of homestead property, half of the lakeshore property and half of the money left in the account after probate plus the car? The will said equal, the final Voucher of Probate in which the car was included, and you signed, said equal, plus our father also said you were to receive the car and I was to have equal compensation." She left out the valuable contents she had stolen and was refusing to divide, and she wasn't finished. She continued to try and control events at the family home. Alison had allergies, she explained, and shouldn't be exposed to Vickie's dog. She finished the letter with, "I have only been trying to give you a factual accounting of the house. I care about you."

She certainly had a funny way of showing it. Her "factual accounting" had greed and possessiveness written all over it.

Brad knew I was plagued with tunnel vision and unable to see the big picture so he, once again, told me his analysis. "Julie has bigger plans. She simply wants to see you have nothing so she can get the house for utilities and tax bills she would pay on your behalf."

Brad's comment left me with feelings of anger, disbelief, and deep emotional pain that a beloved sister could sink to this level.

If he was right, stealing out of the house was just a small part of her overall plot.

Brad continued, "The way I see it, Julie makes you pay room and board, pay full expenses at the parental home instead of offering to pro rate expenses based on use, and insists you pay for a car your father had given you. She then took over expenses at the house instead of selling as you had asked. Even selling the lakeshore property so far below its value, with no thought for your desperate financial situation, was all geared to make you penniless and impotent at the family property. Worse still, the car's engine failed because they didn't change the oil for two years. It was thick and gummy when I checked it. The transmission had gone out and the motor had to be replaced the first four hundred miles you had used the car. You were ill and hadn't driven that much. A used car dealer would have given you a better deal. I hate to say this, but Julie is a master manipulator and one of the most convincing liars I have ever encountered, even in my work! She wants the house, and she wants herself and her girls to inherit the valuables, not you. That is why she is protecting them instead of dividing them, and, by the way, no car or organ has to appear on any Probate."

I listened to his comments. It was

logical but hard to accept. My ex-husband had a broad background in his investigative work and was able to see and understand the implications of others' behaviors far better than I could at this point in my illness. When I reflected on my father and his concern over the car, I was sure I had understood him correctly: he had "given" me the car. When I mentioned this to Brad, he said, "I also understood from your Dad you were to have the car, but Julie will do what she wants." He added, "Julie has been in control of everything for a long time, through your illness and due to you living more than eight hours away, and absolute power corrupts absolutely."

Was Julie aware of her arsenal of negative behaviors? Probably not, I reasoned, since they had most likely developed surreptitiously over the years, to be used with impunity to achieve her objectives when necessary. A formidable and unscrupulous arsenal clothed in dignity, seductive charm, and aristocratic bearing. I was beginning to see that my sister exaggerated benign occurrences to get me on the defensive and galvanize her family and others to her side.

Before answering her letter, I spoke to Vickie. She assured me Alison wasn't allergic to most dogs but mostly cats. I contacted my niece and she assured me that was the case.

Because I wanted to also be accurate in any future discussions written or verbal with my sister, I saved all Julie's letters and copies of my replies. I began keeping a diary and wrote down previous and present interactions so there would be as accurate a record as possible of all that had transpired. Would a well person perceive her behavior differently from what I was experiencing? Only time and recovery would tell.

Three weeks after Julie sent her letter, she called to make sure she had been thoroughly understood in her latest communication. Why couldn't she leave me alone? She controlled everything—why did she feel the need to keep bugging me? In a superior tone, she said, "If you had asked at any time, you would have been informed about how the finances were divided."

"As Representative, it is your job to keep me informed. You have never mentioned to me or your family that you were to have equal compensation. Do you have a conscience, Julie?"

"Well, you signed the probate voucher," she announced triumphantly. "Don't you understand what the letter says?"

"I understand exactly what you are saying," I replied, then read the letter out loud to reinforce the fact.

Julie exploded. This last letter had not been her finest hour, and she knew her bad behavior had been caught, in writing. "You what? You mean you keep all my letters?" I assured her quietly that I did and let Julie know I was surprised that she didn't.

The full scope of Julie's deceit and manipulation was still not clear to me. One month later, I wrote her a letter which, in retrospect, made it obvious I was unaware of the extent of her stealing and deceit. My goal was to be conciliatory yet firm. "One thing I feel sure about, Dad would not have wanted you to feel cheated, nor do I."

Julie knew I hated fighting and always took the path of least resistance. Her attitude was always one of assertiveness with friends, but around family she acted aggressively but clothed her actions in passivity while achieving her goals.

My letter continued, "However, I am equally sure Dad would have honored his promise of "equal cash" to me and would not have wanted, without my knowledge, the money extracted from me at a time when I am still a hardship case and certainly not in a way that causes me to be a partner without privileges at the house."

I encouraged Julie to keep the letters between us "as a crutch for recall so there will be no further misunderstandings."

I addressed the issue regarding Alison: "The 'jockeying for position' comment I made was not disrespect to your family, but an attempt to force you to look at yourself. Why are you jockeying for power and position at the house? Why can't we enjoy and happily share the house? I feel that fine line of respect was crossed last summer with the bed incident."

I also made my opinions known about Alison's allergies. I didn't know at the time that Liz also had a dog and frequently brought it to the parental home. I finished the letter with, "I feel you disregard anything I tell you. Your opinions and beliefs, in your eyes, seem to be the only right ones. I have worked for nine years teaching people to communicate more effectively but feel my efforts to communicate with you about anything are a dismal failure. I have never tried so hard and failed so miserably. It seems you view nothing I have ever said as positive or accurate or as an appropriate response to any given circumstances. I feel badly it has come to this." I merely signed my initial.

A week later, Alison called, very upset. She said, "My mother read the parts of your letter she wanted the family to hear the evening we were all there. She and Liz convulsed with laughter and made derogatory comments about your failure in your attempts to communicate. The rest of us sensed how desperately you were trying to be conciliatory with my mother and find common ground. As the laughter continued and nasty comments abounded, all of us except Liz left the room. We were all disgusted."

THIRTEEN

MORE REVELATIONS

1991 - 1992

Brad and I spent Thanksgiving 1991 in Illinois with Vickie. The Christmas season was in full swing, and Brad and I did some Christmas shopping. We would be spending Christmas at home in Springfield. Vickie planned to spend four days with us.

Brad picked up a tree and together he and I decorated it. We wrapped gifts and planned the holiday meal. All preparations were complete when Vickie arrived, her car full of gifts, luggage, and dogs. Despite all the contentiousness that had marked the fall, our spirits were high. I had sent gifts to Julie and her family. Julie returned her gift, saying she couldn't accept it but Liz wrote a thank you note for her family and Alison called to thank Brad and me and had a long conversation with Vickie.

After the holidays, Aunt Doris called to

inquire about my health and asked me if I really kept all Julie's letters. I explained I wanted to make sure I responded appropriately to Julie's remarks and had decided to keep them. Aunt Doris was unaware of the symptoms of ME/CFS. I wasn't sure what kind of information Julie had given our aunt. She went on to say, "Well, some people might consider that vicious."

"It was not, at all, meant that way."

Aunt Doris didn't press the issue and went on to other topics and news about her family, then stated, "I understood from your dad you were to be given the car and half the cash."

I was surprised and pleased that Aunt Doris also knew. "I have to pay for the car."

"Why?"

"Julie wants to be paid." I didn't reveal that Brad had put a new motor in the car because they never changed the oil. Aunt Doris was silent. *God forbid if she should ever criticize her favorite niece.*

After we hung up, I was struck to think that Dad had spoken to two people about the car. He was an honest man, and I felt more certain of what he had related to me: "Take it, it's yours! You will get your half of the money." Julie hadn't sent the title to be signed over to me most likely on purpose.

Even if the car had been signed over, I now suspected she would have surreptitiously extracted the money from the estate.

Over the rest of the winter months, Julie and I had no more communication and I hoped that with time and a cooling-off period, the situation between us might improve. I continued to suffer symptoms but with less intensity. Wishing I had a better memory, I still didn't connect it to the illness.

When spring arrived, Julie plotted with Liz to invite Vickie to meet them halfway between their homes at a mall for a day of shopping.

Vickie accepted their offer. Alison called later to tell Vickie that Julie and Liz were plotting to turn her against me. She didn't want any part of it and in the meantime, Vickie invited a friend to + accompany her. She called us and told us that her Aunt Julie's plots were not worthy of her standing in the community and church. She said, "I know one thing for sure. They have never offered to meet me before, and I have to ask, 'Why now?'"

Vickie and her friend, Margie, set out on the appointed day and met Julie and Liz. They had lunch together and shopped then left to come home. Vickie called when she reached home to talk about her day with her aunt and cousin. "No attempt was made to get me to talk derogatorily about you. Aunt Julie needs a job. She's got too much time on her hands...." She added, "She needs an exorcism to get the evil out!"

*   *   *   *   *

In early spring, Brad's brother Bill called and asked that Brad come home to assist in the roofing of the summer kitchen at my parents' home. Brad spoke with Julie and told her we wanted to stay at the house. As usual, she said she and Jim planned to come around the same time. This meant we were banished to Brad's family farm, where roughing it was the norm. The house was heated by an old-fashioned, woodburning stove in the dining room and a small oil burner in the living room. There was no heat upstairs and the bedrooms had to be heated by opening the hall door. This was late May, so the weather was still cool.

Brad started the fires and it took all day and most of the evening for the walls to warm as the place had been shut down all winter with no heat. The water on the farm was hard and from a well. We needed purified, reverse osmosis water to drink and cook, so bottles of water were brought in. I slept in Brad's mother's bed downstairs, which was the most comfortable and the bathroom was nearby. Any laundry needs entailed a trip to the laundromat in town.

With reflection on the circumstances between myself and my sister for what might have been, it made me sad. My parents' home, with a few changes, could have easily accommodated all of us and yet there was this tug of war and, as Brad called it, "Squatters' Rights mentality". Through the years, we had been such a close family. It would have been such fun to be together, but after Dad died, things did change—Vickie was right about that. How would it all be resolved?

When Bill and Brad finished the roofing job over the summer kitchen, Bill commented that the house needed a new roof and promised to do it the following summer. Sadly, he passed away from lung cancer the following year. Brad gave Julie the bill for materials. I was never sure whether our joint account paid for the materials or whether Jim, who had a better sense of fairness than Julie, paid for the materials since Brad and Bill had provided the labor. I wasn't willing to ask Julie and be on the receiving end of her hostility.

I took advantage of this trip to, once again, visit Aunt Beckie. Vickie and I arrived at the long-term care facility and my aunt's doctor came in later. I spoke to him about how Beckie was doing as she hadn't recognized me right away. He said, "Your aunt doesn't seem to remember friends at all for the last six months and, in that time, she doesn't seem to know Julie or me either."

Aunt Beckie had known her doctor since he was a little boy. I had been his classmate and we had been best friends.

I noticed Aunt Beckie was failing physically and seemed, at times, withdrawn. She would however hold my hand the entire time we visited. After a few days of regular visits, Aunt Beckie knew who I was.

The day I left, I hugged and kissed her goodbye and said I would be back the Fourth of July. Aunt Beckie did not seem to absorb or respond to this bit of information, yet she hugged me so tight I felt she would never let me go. It was always so painful to leave her.

After Brad and I returned to Illinois, we received an invitation to attend Kerry's daughter's wedding near the hometown on Memorial Day weekend. The whole family would be there, so I thought I would take a chance that Julie could be civil and called her to reserve a time at the parental home.

"Are you going to use the house the week before the Memorial Day wedding or the week after?"

"We are using the house both weeks. We *always* use the house from May 15th to July 17th. Alison and Dan use the house in August, so you are just going to have to call."

Julie finished in a nasty, imperious voice. I recalled in that moment that she had endlessly complained about their former co-owners of their two-bedroom condo in Florida when they acted like this. Now she was doing it to me!

"Then," I replied matter-of-factly, "if you are using the house that much, perhaps we should pro rate the expenses based on use. In the months neither of us use the house, we would share the expenses. In other words, add up the total expenses for the year, keep a calendar when the house is in use and by whom, and pro rate from there. I will call you when I want to use it and you inform me when you use it."

"Absolutely not!" Julie shot back. "I don't have to tell you anything, but you had better tell *me* if you use the house!" The conversation ended shortly thereafter.

When I related the conversation to Brad, he told me I should have been informed every time they entered the house and vice versa. He also confirmed that my nieces' use of the house should not supersede mine. Later, I noticed I was no longer being charged for electric, gas, or telephone at the house. When the bills arrived, they were for my part of the water-sewer bill, taxes, and any maintenance. Since she would not discuss much with me, I had to wonder if the expenses they did take made up for what wasn't included. I should have had the courage to ask but in my present state felt I was still too slow and couldn't handle conflict.

Vickie pointed out that I was up against a schemer and manipulator who had spent months, maybe years, perfecting her act while I was concentrating on a regime that would help me regain my health.

When I questioned Brad as to why I had to pay the full water bill and taxes when they used the house so extensively, Brad suggested Jim must be taking at least some of the utilities as a write-off, as he sometimes conducted business in the hometown and surrounding areas. He strongly doubted they were doing this out of the goodness of their hearts. He added, "No judge would let Julie get away with what she is doing. Tenants-in-Common should be taking turns for holidays and share their times more fairly."

About three weeks before Kerry's daughter's wedding, Aunt Doris called to offer me a place to sleep as the wedding was near her home. My parents' place was two hours east, and since my previous plan had been thwarted, I was grateful for Aunt Doris' offer. She said she wanted to make sure I had a comfortable bed. I was touched by the offer, quickly accepted, and thanked her. Brad and Vickie would stay with Brad's sister, who lived near Doris.

I had nothing to wear. I had gone from a size 6 to a 10. I never dressed up anymore, but on one of my better days Brad took me to shop. As appalled at myself as I was, the situation couldn't be controlled. ME/CFS patients were advised not to try to diet as they would probably feel worse. The shopping went well. I chose a dark blue dress with a yellow jacket in order to hide the weight gain. Despite trying to look decent, I was sure I looked frumpy.

The day before Memorial Day weekend, we packed to leave for Aunt Doris's and we picked up Vickie. Brad made a bed in the back of the car for me, and Vickie helped drive. Once we arrived, I felt decent enough.

We changed clothes and left for the church and the late afternoon wedding. As we arrived, we could see Jim and Julie's car down the line from us in the same row. My nieces and their husbands exited from other cars. They had apparently been waiting for Julie and Jim to arrive and they started toward the church together.

We exited from our car. Julie could not have helped see us, but never spoke even though I watched her carefully. Jim nodded to Brad and me somberly. Alison and Liz turned and waved as they headed for the church. The wedding was a lovely affair and after the ceremony, the reception was held at a country club.

I did not see my sister again until we arrived at the reception. Our tables had been placed next to each other. Jim and Julie sat with their backs to our table. My nieces and their husbands were seated with them. Brad, with a twinkle in his eye, pulled out the chairs facing their table and were joined by Vickie and a few more distant relatives. After the meal, Alison and Liz came over to the table and hugged both Brad and me as they exchanged pleasantries. Vickie didn't feel as cordial toward her Aunt Julie, but Brad and I encouraged her to be polite and pleasant. The rest of the evening went smoothly and the next day we returned home.

* * * * *

Feeling stronger, I began walking in the warm spring air a few times a week, tolerating about fifteen minutes. I also resumed back exercises. My poor memory persisted. Slowly, I was able to connect events to Julie's surreptitious behavior. Could I see and understand the full picture? I knew I couldn't.

FOURTEEN

MEMORIES SURFACE

1992

Near the Fourth of July, the three of us returned to the hometown. Julie and Jim were already at the house. There had been no contact with my sister. We settled in at Brad's family farm. Vickie and I went to visit Aunt Beckie. She seemed bright and knew us right away. She asked how I was getting along with my sister. "She doesn't share very well," I replied. "I have not gotten anything I'm supposed to have."

"Just remember, they are only material things." Aunt Beckie squeezed my hand.

"But it's not always about material things. It's about being treated this way…it hurts so much. We were so close—how could she do this?"

"I know," my aunt replied sympathetically.

I had brought my aunt a box of candy, which she couldn't get enough of, and she thanked us profusely. A nurse approached me and told me Aunt Beckie had never been out of the care center since she entered a year and a half ago. I was shocked at the information and asked Vickie if she could help. She quickly agreed.

We dressed my aunt warmly and Vickie wheeled her out. We proceeded to walk through the neighborhood. Aunt Beckie's former home was nearby, and Vickie and I took her past. I had lived there with my aunt for a time while in high school. Aunt Beckie could not recall the house, but she seemed really alert. When we walked by a large, white church, without any prodding, she said that was where she had spent many hours—and she was right. She had directed the choir at the church, sometimes filled in as organist, held her piano recitals there, and I had been in the choir and performed in the piano recitals.

I held tightly to Aunt Beckie's hand and we began to sing all the old songs we used to sing together. If anyone heard us, they would probably have thought we were crazy, but I didn't care. This was so special. When we returned to the center, there was a religious service going on and we sat through it, continuing to hold hands. It broke my heart I was not well enough to care for her. Aunt Beckie leaned over and confided, "We have always had such a deep love for each other, haven't we?" I agreed and gave her a hug. Each day we were in town, we visited her and either took her for a walk or sat together on the patio. One of the days we visited, Aunt Beckie asked how I was getting along with Julie.

"She doesn't share very well," I repeated.

"You'll probably get cheated. She is cheating me too, but I'm too old to fight." She then spoke about her missing bonds of $4000 that she had signed over to Jim that had never been placed in her checking account as she had requested. Jim was honest but had probably given them to Julie. If they had been signed over to Jim, nothing could be done about it anyway.

I decided Aunt Beckie should be taken out of the facility for a day. Hopefully, something could be arranged at the family home which would allow her to leave the unit for a little while for dinner and some social interaction with the family. Vickie and I drove to the house and my aunt waited in the car while I went inside to speak to Jim and Julie—and pick up some of my belongings I had recently been able to remember. Julie would probably be on her best behavior with Jim there.

On arrival, I asked them if they would

be open to Aunt Beckie spending an afternoon at the house on July Fourth. Brad, of course, would be there to help. Jim and Julie looked at each other for a long moment, which gave me a strange feeling something wasn't right. Then, Jim turned to me: "No, we have no way to get her up the steps without a ramp."

"Couldn't we just pull the wheelchair backwards, one step at a time? With two men, there would be plenty of strength and Aunt Beckie is a small woman."

"I don't think it is safe to try," Jim insisted firmly. Disappointed, they seemed resistant to doing it anytime.

Then, I changed the subject: "I want to get the key ring from Mother and Dad's room that I gave Mother one Christmas. Her initials make up the ring." Julie, not speaking, went to her handbag and rummaged through it as I started for my parents' bedroom. I went to the closet where I knew Mother had kept her luggage and the key ring, but noticed Jim followed me into the room and stood, watching. When Julie walked in, Jim left. Julie came over to watch as I pulled the key ring from Mother's luggage with, "Oh, yes, here it is." Julie looked pleasantly surprised and merely smiled. I continued, "By the way, the red Swiss knife you gave Jim was my gift to Dad." Julie looked shocked. "It's alright though," I added. "Jim may have the knife."

She still said nothing and failed to thank me. There was something in the upstairs closet I wanted to retrieve and told her as much as she followed me up the steps.

I collected my jewelry box and said, "Do you remember that this is mine?" Julie nodded in the affirmative without speaking.

When I returned to the car, I was dismayed. "Do you know they followed me everywhere I went in the house?" I said to Vickie. "If they are this distrustful of me, no wonder Julie didn't want me to have a key. I never realized it was about stealing! All this time, I thought it was about control. I'd never stolen in my life, except once at age eight when I stole a silver ribbon from a girlfriend. I thought it was the most beautiful thing I had ever seen, but felt so terrible, I returned it the next day. I never wanted to experience that feeling again. Later, when I told Brad, he said, "Do you remember about your dad's gun?" I said no and he reminded me; "Jim was to have the grill. I was to have your grandfather's gun because your grandfather hunted on our farm with my family for years. Your dad wanted Jim to have the gun because he was the son-in-law, and I told Abbie to do that, but she kept insisting she wanted me to have it, that it was her father's gun, and it should be her choice who received it. That's the last I heard about it."

"Yes, I think I do remember. The grill and the gun. Mother made it very clear. We were all sitting in the kitchen: Julie, Jim, you, Mother, Dad, and I. They went through all the designated items. That was when Mother had the old kitchen table against the wall instead of in the center of the room, right?" Brad silently nodded in assent. I was flushed with revelation. Events sometimes came back even though recall was slow. "I'm going to mention it to Julie the next time I see her."

Brad disagreed. "Naw, I would very much like to have it to add to my collection, but she probably gave it to Jim, so let him have it." Later we found out she had given it to her son-in-law as Jim didn't hunt.

* * * * *

The Fourth of July weekend dawned with a clear, cloudless sky and a bright, warm sun—a perfect day with the temperature in the mid-seventies and a wonderful, light breeze off the lake. Brad and I sat outside on lawn chairs, where we had full view of the fields, now cropless, planted with switchgrass and flowers, the orchard, and the woods. The old red brick house sat back from the road, connected by a long lane. There were two barns in the barnyard, no longer housing horses, cows, pigs, chickens, and Guinea hens—just tractors and old hay. The barnyard was no longer bare but was covered with grass, extending the lawn.

As we sat there that morning, sipping our coffee, we saw a six-point buck peering at us through the foliage of the orchard. He was magnificent and watched us for a long while before he wandered off. A little later, a young coyote stealthily crossed the barnyard disappearing into the tall grass. It was so peaceful, a healing respite from the last contact with Julie.

Brad began to talk about his remembrances from a different time when growing up on the farm. His father had inherited the farm but wasn't a particularly industrious farmer. He was known for his honesty when he had to borrow money to pay dental bills and for Brad's emergency surgery for appendicitis. People readily lent him the money because they knew he would pay them back.

Brad was the youngest of seven children, five boys and two girls, all born on the farm. He and his brothers and sisters walked to the country school. Brad took a potato to school for his lunch, heated it on the schoolroom stove that heated the classroom. He always wore hand-me-downs, even his shoes. The first new pair of shoes he had was for his graduation from high school, but he wore his brother's suit under his gown.

The five sons helped work the farm. Brad said he started picking stones and pulling weeds when he was ten years old as they couldn't afford the machinery to do the job. By the time he was twelve, he was driving a tractor and plowing.

When Brad's father was killed in an accident, the funeral was the biggest the town had ever seen. As the hearse made its way to the cemetery, the line of cars was one-and one-half miles long, bumper to bumper.

For the first time, I was able to add to Brad's memories with a few of my own. His mother had been the daughter of a prosperous farmer, had a teaching certificate and, as a young girl, a horse and buggy of her own. One of his sisters once told me how they went to school all day and, "Mother held school all evening. We got a double dose."

When I was dating Brad, I was amazed at her normal day. She began baking at dawn before going to the barn and milking six cows. She prepared three meals a day for nine people, plus did her housekeeping chores. She had a washer but no dryer, so she hung out clothes to dry. When I was there, she asked what my favorite dessert was. Of course, it was chocolate cake with her white fluffy frosting, for which I now wished I had the recipe.

Eventually, Vickie joined Brad and me and we planned our day. We had decided to rest and try to do the flea market tomorrow. Our only activity would be to visit Aunt Beckie this afternoon. After breakfast, we sat in the sun and just relaxed.

Saturday dawned as beautiful as Friday. Once again, we visited Aunt Beckie, then headed for the flea market. Brad was not interested and chose to visit friends he had known since high school.

Vickie and I arrived at the flea market in the early afternoon and ate lunch before we proceeded to view the vendor booths. I tired well before Vickie and sat down on a bench. Vickie found a vendor who sold our favorite shower gels and creams and came back to the bench to tell me. I forced myself to walk to the booth and bought some. By afternoon, I had found some wooden spatulas for cooking and two beautiful pins, one with blue stones and the other the color of salmon. They were old and heavy, perfect for my collection.

After I returned to the bench, I was approached by some old friends, Laurie and Jake. It was a pleasant surprise to see they had come across the county for the market. I invited them to come out to the farm for dinner and they enthusiastically accepted the invitation.

Brad and Jake sat outside, attending to the grilled chicken breasts. Vickie and I had prepared potato salad ahead of time and we cooked asparagus then added a fresh veggie plate with a dill dip. It was an easy but tasty dinner. Laurie and Jake seemed to thoroughly enjoy it. Eventually, Laurie asked why we were at the farm instead of at the house in town. She had never met my sister. I felt safe in being open with her. When I explained about not being allowed to use the house, she added a story of her own.

Her oldest brother had been executor of her family estate. All went well, but when he told her she could enter the locked house to get the things that were designated to her, his wife followed her throughout the house. She said it gave her a very unsettling feeling.

"Did they think I was going to steal? It really made the process painful for me. The only thing I didn't get was my mother's China cabinet. My brother wanted it for his son and had already put it on his truck. As it turned out, the house Jake and I bought was so small I had no dining room, and my living room wouldn't have accommodated it. I got the money I was supposed to receive and, unlike you, all was over in two years.

Silently, I noted the difference between her experience and mine. We were past probate, had tenants-in-common in place, the house stripped of all valuables, and I was still followed through the house. We talked about so much that evening that we missed going to the fireworks.

Sunday morning dawned another beautiful day but somewhat cooler. We planned to go into town for the parade, but with the wind off the lake, we took our jackets. There was never enough music in this parade to please me. When I last attended other parades in nearby towns, they always managed to have several floats with music. This one was full of firetrucks, tractors, and winners from the tractor pulls held the night before. Businesses advertised with a few floats, some with trucks carrying signs with clever phrases and only one float had music. We saw some residents we knew, and it was an enjoyable time despite the mediocre parade.

A few days later, Faith called at the farm as she had heard through Julie that we were in town for the holiday. "How are you doing?" she asked after greetings.

"I feel I'm slowly improving."

"Did you see your Aunt Beckie?"

"Yes, Vickie and I have spent almost every day with her, and we took her outside. She loved it."

"I wonder if you knew Jim and Julie gave a huge party on the Fourth. Your Aunt Doris was there, her kids and their spouses, and a lot of people I didn't know. I was there to help with the party."

"I wanted to bring Aunt Beckie up for the day, but they refused. That was probably why." I wondered why they couldn't have been honest and just set another date instead of making up stupid excuses.

"I have been upset over Bob's story to me about your sister and Jim checking the house after you left," Faith went on. "There was another incident you might want to know about. A friend of your mother's brought her a freshly baked pie in a beautiful glass pie plate with a matching cover. After a weekend visit by Julie and Jim, the friend returned to retrieve her pie plate. It had completely disappeared from the house. Your mother called and we searched everywhere. We turned the kitchen upside down. Abbie was so upset and embarrassed. I felt sorry for her. Later, I happened to be working at the house and heard them talking. I got the impression your parents had pieced together the total picture. There seemed to be other things missing."

I thanked her for the information and told her about my encounter with them when they followed me all over the house. Faith was aghast. The conversation ended shortly thereafter with Faith asking me to call her the next time we visited. I couldn't help but be touched by Faith's concern. I hadn't had much contact with her and felt Julie knew her better and relied a lot on Faith. As soon as she hung up, I burst into tears. I felt such grief over my mother's upset and embarrassment. I cried over this terminally ill woman who was put through this. How long had Julie been like this? It was just one more insight into Julie's dark side. Is that why she thought I was stealing, doing to her what she was doing to me? I wasn't yet ready or able to confront her, but my resolve had not dimmed. There was so much I knew I couldn't conceive of regarding Julie's plots and manipulations. How long had she been like this? For years, and we just didn't notice?

* * * * *

We returned to Illinois and settled into our usual routines. My daily walks increased to twenty minutes and my symptoms, now mild, were occurring every six to eight weeks. Brad was supportive. There was no communication with my sister.

The summer faded into a fall suffused with deep greens, golds, and reds along with cool clear air. The beauty on my daily walks reminded me of my mother and how she had loved the fall colors. Then, a happy memory came to mind. One fall I had requested some cattails and large thistles. Mom and Aunt Beckie had lovingly and excitedly tramped "the flats", an area near the lake that was very damp with some sparse woods, in order to get them for me. They painted them with golds and silvers and gave them to me at Thanksgiving. I used them to accent a holiday bouquet of dried flowers I always prepared near the holidays. It didn't occur to me that I had just recalled a memory from the past. It would be another several weeks before the real awakening began.

* * * * *

Brad was out of town periodically on police business. It was often three to four days a week. It was during one of his absences, five years from the date of the onset of the ME/CFS, that memories I had been unable to recall finally began to surface. It started one morning while I was quietly drinking my morning coffee and went on for three devastating days. Memories kept surfacing, unbidden, one memory after another, tumbling into my consciousness. As each memory surfaced, I found myself in wonderment, sometimes in tears...

Slowly, I recalled childhood memories. Alison had thought Julie's resentments were from early childhood. Did she have a point? Maybe Julie never outgrew her resentments and childhood behaviors—but she had been a wonderful sister for thirty years. If Alison was right, what was the cause?

My thoughts turned to Mom. I could now remember her telling me that I had been born sickly. She had walked the floor with me during the day as I cried almost constantly, pulling my legs up as if in pain. Dad would come home from work and walk or rock me while Mom got some sleep and cooked dinner. She was often up during the night with a crying baby. They feared I would never live to grow into adulthood. Finally, I was diagnosed on the verge of ricketts. Did all that attention alienate Julie for the rest of our lives?

Aunt Beckie had lived with us because her husband was ill and hospitalized much of the time. She gave each of us attention, taking Julie with her on short trips, teaching her how to carry a tune, how to play the piano. She rocked me and sang to me and let me button and unbutton her sweater. Whatever had happened to Julie, apparently all the loving attention wasn't enough. Could she now openly express her hatred of me because Mom and Dad were gone?

The recall continued: With all the concern for the new baby, enough was enough for my five-year-old sister and, on a hot August day, she donned her winter cap, packed a small suitcase reserved for her doll clothes, and with undaunted determination walked three long blocks to her maternal grandparents' home, discreetly followed by our father. Later that day, Dad arrived to claim his daughter, but the grandparents talked him out of it when Julie took up an irretrievable position under a double bed in the back bedroom. Three weeks later, after a lot of coaxing, Julie finally agreed to return home.

The physical problems continued. I had multiple surgeries and was diagnosed with Bright's disease. Fortunately, the recovery left me with minimal kidney damage.

When Julie was eight, she began to harass me in various ways. On one occasion, my mother heard soft, muffled yells coming from the upstairs bedroom. Quietly, Mom climbed the stairs and found Julie attempting to force me to read. When I couldn't, she threw me on the bed and covered my head with a pillow! Mom intervened and I was spared to endure further torture at the hands of my sister.

When I was five, my friend Sharon and I would play together and Julie would join us from time to time. My sister always had to make all the rules in our play and Sharon would get angry and go home. One day, as each of us took turns in a swing that hung from a big tree in the yard, Julie dared me to swear. "Oh, come on. Say 'shit'. I dare you. You are a chicken. Besides, I won't tell Mother. Come on! See? I swear," and proudly added "Shit!"

"Shit," I echoed.

"Oh! I'm going to tell Mother what you said!" Julie ran for the house to tattle.

Mom came out the back door, descended purposefully down the porch steps, and with a determined gait made her way toward me. "Did you swear?"

I looked at my sister, who was smiling triumphantly just out of Mother's range of vision, and said hesitantly, "Well, Julie told me to. She swore too."

"No I didn't! She's lying!" Julie protested.

"Well, if she told you to jump into Lake Huron, would you?"

I shrugged. "No, but—"

Mom grabbed my arm and marched me into the house. "Children who swear get their mouths washed out with soap!" she announced.

"But Julie swore too," I cried.

Julie, who was right on our heels, basking in the light of her deceit, insisted in a very adamant and convincing voice, "No, I didn't. She's lying, Mother!"

"If Julie were swearing too, she wouldn't be telling on you," Mother reasoned erroneously.

That evening at dinner we had mashed potatoes. Julie sat directly across the table from me on the other side of Dad. When no one was looking, she would stick out her tongue heaped with half-chewed food, and I would look away to avoid nausea. When I would peek at her she would smirk.

Despite her behavior toward me, I loved, adored, and looked up to my sister. She tried to get away with as much as she could—she was fearless, rebellious, and triumphant over her occasional successes.

When she played dolls with Sharon and me, she insisted we had to begin by dividing up the dolls. Julie would always shout, "First choice!" If by some quirk of fate Sharon or I thought to say "First choice" first, Julie would tell us with great authority that we had done it wrong and so we would have to say "First choice" again. Then, without drawing a breath, she would finish with "First choice!". When one or both of us objected, Julie would reply in her queenly manner, "But you did it wrong and I have first choice!" One day, Sharon shouted angrily as tears began to stream down her cheeks: "You always do that, change the rules to suit yourself! If you don't give me first choice, I'm going home!"

"That's the way it is, Sharon," Julie replied.

Sharon left for home crying. Julie muttered something about what a bad mood Sharon was in and added she probably needed a nap. When we got home, Sharon's mother had called. Mom questioned my sister, but as usual, Julie had an explanation that Sharon was just being fretful and difficult. Mother dropped it after asking me. I said Julie hadn't done anything wrong because I wanted to win my sister's elusive approval. It never occurred to me to stand up to her.

When I was eight, my dad wanted to take a break from his job as superintendent. When school was out that spring, we moved to another town and my parents bought a small home in a new subdivision. Dad took a job as a supervisor and worked 3-11. Mom started beauty school because she wanted to have her own business. That meant when school started, Mom would be taking her classes and Dad would be home to get us off to school. When we returned from school, Julie, now a freshman, had charge of me until Mom returned. She would also babysit me on Saturday mornings while our parents did the weekly shopping.

I always had a thousand projects planned, including practicing tap dancing and piano, and this Saturday morning was no exception. A friend was coming over, but she couldn't come until my chores were done. Hurriedly, I cleaned the bathroom sink and toilet, straightened the bathroom, picked up my side of the room, made my bed, and practiced my piano. Julie was reading a teen magazine, wasting time posing in the bathroom mirror, and talking to a friend on the phone. When she hung up and saw I had my chores done, she marched over to my bed and tore it up, then dumped bottles from the medicine cabinet onto my bed. "You can't play yet! Put these things away and make your bed!"

Hurt and frustration welled up inside me. I fell to my knees with my head on the bed and sobbed. My sister was always harassing me. Teary-eyed and without looking, I tossed the bottles angrily on my sister's unmade bed instead of putting them away as instructed. I re-made my bed and went to the basement to play and practice dancing. I didn't try to call my friend.

When our parents came home, my sister told them I had thrown a bottle at her because she told me to make my bed and showed them a mark on the wall where the bottle supposedly had hit. I was stunned, she hadn't been in the room when I threw the bottles on the bed! Mom chose to believe Julie, perhaps because she knew I had a temper, but failed to take into consideration I was not a rebellious child. Julie watched triumphantly from the door of our room as Mom put me over her knee and gave me three whacks on the behind. It didn't hurt, but I cried from frustration.

With all the trauma going on, I adjusted poorly to our new life and school where a boy from class began following me home. I told the teachers but nothing was done. Then he began waiting outside the girls' restroom. Finally, the teachers noticed and put a stop to it. The only bright light that awful year was a great aunt, my maternal grandmother's sister, who was warm, loving, funny, and fun to be around. My parents sensed I was happy around her and made sure we visited her often. It helped relieve the terrible loss I felt with Aunt Beckie no longer in my life. Julie had made the comment that I had failed the third grade and she may have been right, but I had a report card with all A's and was told I had rated extremely high on the achievement tests. I went on to the fourth grade.

After Dad's conference with the teacher, however, and whatever had transpired, he decided to return to our hometown and resume his position as superintendent. Dad and I would return together, and Julie would remain behind with Mom while she finished her course in beauty school.

Dad and I lived with my paternal grandparents. I loved my grandmother, our "happy Grandma," but my grandfather was rather stern. In contrast, my maternal grandfather rocked me, gently kidded me, and made me laugh a lot. I was back with my beloved Aunt Beckie and my maternal grandmother whom I adored. It would be a yearlong sabbatical from Julie until the harassment would resume.

When Mom and Julie came home, Julie was rebellious throughout her last two years of high school. She constantly broke curfew and fought with Mom. I hated the conflict. In my adolescent years, my sister became adept at procrastination or stonewalling. This was Julie's most potent tactic when she wanted to assert her power over Mom. She could hook her into angry responses, which seemed to please her.

When no one was around, Julie would hit me in the most tender part of my body, my newly developing breasts. When I complained, Julie denied it. Mom's assessment? "Your sister may try to tease you occasionally, but she isn't mean." Her response to Julie was, "Be more careful around Josie."

Our mother was now home all the time and Julie acted out less frequently. Mom had opened her own beauty shop in our home, the second downstairs bedroom. As a result, I returned to my happy, busy self.

Despite Julie successfully manipulating and charming our mother, she had positive attributes as well. There was one incident I will never forget.

We lived near one of the Great Lakes and on one warm, bright summer day, Julie and a friend Marge decided to go swimming. Marge was not a strong swimmer. My sister was strong and very athletic. After a while, an unpredictably forceful offshore wind began and Marge, who had an inflatable doughnut, began drifting farther and farther from shore. As she drifted dangerously far offshore, my sister, who had taken swimming and lifesaving in Phys. Ed., set out to bring her in. Julie reached Marge about three quarters of a mile from shore and brought her in. There was praise all around for her heroic effort. The entire town heard about it and Julie had endless admirers.

Julie was a good student, and a high scorer on the girls' basketball team. She was the beauty of the family and in her last year of high school was chosen beauty queen.

Julie attended private college, our father's alma mater. It was a stretch for my parents, but they agreed and bought her many beautiful clothes and away she went. After she left for college, I never lost or misplaced another item. She attended college one semester, went to work, and then entered nurses' training. She continued to play basketball and was star player of the nurses' league. After she finished, she worked for a year and became engaged.

She made wedding plans and reluctantly asked me to be maid of honor at Mother's strong urging. I remembered with pleasure that Julie and I became friends for the first time in our lives, when I was about twenty years old. We began to have true moments of closeness. She was kind, thoughtful, extremely warm and charming and even loving toward me. All the old behaviors seemed to have been matured through. I assumed my sister had outgrown the meanness and rivalry she felt as a child. I always admired and loved her and was deeply touched by her acceptance of me as a beloved sister. We called each other frequently and shared our thoughts and feelings with a closeness I never dreamed we could achieve. Was Alison right? Had our relationship been a superficial one for her all these years, or was there another explanation?

That evening when I spoke of my recall

to Brad on the phone as he was still out of town, I wondered out loud if perhaps Julie hadn't outgrown the childhood experiences and they had a bearing on her behavior now. Brad, in his easy going way, answered, "No. Julie plots and plans and is controlling. She's trying to justify it. You just don't fit in with her grand design. I blame your parents. They never stopped the behavior."

Thoughts of my mother came back to me. She had always been so loving to both of us. I missed my parents and their loving concern for me. My world was so different now, trying to deal with Julie. My mother always worried about my situation and often expressed as much. Occasionally she offered to give me money, but I refused. Ten years into her illness, she asked me to take a trip with her as Dad no longer wanted to travel. When we went to Williamsburg, we spent a lot of hours together and she spoke about her fears of becoming incapacitated as well as her concerns about me.

"You were always such a happy little girl and life has not been kind to you. I worry about you."

Often, near the end of her life, I cried myself to sleep in those last months. No matter how old or how sick a loved one may be, we are never ready to give them up.

Another episode that I recalled was when Julie had accused me of neglecting Mother: "She never heard from you." Again, I was dull with no recall when accused of this. Now I could remember that I had called Mother when I could but working three to four double shifts a week left me drained in the few hours I had to myself. My neglect had been, in my mind, my absence from their 50th wedding anniversary celebration. I sent a gift and called.

I was beginning to connect the dots. The references Julie made to me after Mother's funeral about how I had left her and Jim at the hospital before her death may have been part of Julie building her case against me. She knew of my lack of vacation time and money problems. It was imperative that I return to work. Dad had seemed okay about my having to leave. *Brad was right,* I concluded. Julie certainly had tried to build a case against me. Was that why she encouraged me not to come to Williamsport during Mother's last hospitalization, then seemed so disgusted when I did? I was upset by Julie's urging, paid no attention to it, and came anyway.

Thoughts continued to surface, hour after hour. Mom disbursed pieces of jewelry and other valuables to us after our maternal and paternal grandparents had passed away. Julie was given our maternal grandfather's gold knife with his name engraved on it, a pearl pen with gold tip of our grandmother's, and an 18K gold pendant watch more splendid than anything else in the family. I was only fourteen at the time, but I was given my maternal grandmother's bracelet and ring. Set aside until later when I was older were my maternal grandfather's 18K gold and diamond ring and my grandmother's gold-filled pendant watch. Mom loved to wear it on occasion. It was kept in her dresser drawer. During the designations, Julie became very upset and demanded angrily, "Well, what am I to have for a man's ring?"

Mom replied, "You may have your father's onyx ring with the diamond chips." Julie said no more but looked displeased. That made sense, I reasoned, and Julie never gave me either item when approached about it. I overheard Julie coaxing Mother to change her mind so she might have the 18K gold ring instead of the onyx one. She argued that, since she had male grandchildren, she should be given all the men's rings. Mom was silent and unyielding to her pleas.

I began to remember scenes regarding the organ. Mother wanted me to have it. Now I could remember that Julie had exploded, "I don't want Aunt Beckie's! I want this one!"

Mom had become upset and said, "If Josie decides she doesn't want it, she cannot sell it, she is to give it to you." Now I understood why I had assumed designated gifts would be given, not bought. With the Tiffany worth around $8000 to $10,000 estate value, that was probably why I had been designated the extra items like the car and victrola. Julie had replied, "I would like your bedroom set if Josie keeps the organ." The bedroom set was a beautiful walnut and maple four-piece set from the early thirties.

Mom announced firmly, "It's not that I have an objection to you having it, but I am not promising anything else!" Her voice was calm and firm, but the expression on her face belied her voice. She was angry, an emotion I seldom saw in my mother. It seemed every time she tried to designate something, Julie objected to what she was to have and could never seem to accept anything graciously.

There was our last Thanksgiving together, a year before Mom died. Julie had insisted all through dinner that Liz should get Mom's best set of dishes. Mom never responded. I didn't react because I had always felt that whatever my mother or Aunt Beckie wanted to give and to whom was their business. Inheritance was not a right, but a gift. After dinner, Mom presented me with her most treasured, imported linen damask tablecloth. Julie flew into a rage, her face contorted. "Why are you giving her THAT CLOTH? YOU KNOW I want that cloth!"

Mom replied calmly, "I have bought you and given you many beautiful things and Josephine deserves some beautiful things too." I handed the cloth back to my mother not wanting to see her treated this way. Mom turned to me, "Now take it! Get it out of here!" She sounded urgent and thrust it into my hands. She turned to Julie, "You may have this cloth, Julie," indicating another older damask cloth wrapped in a roll.

Julie retorted, "I don't like this cloth! I don't want it!" She thrust it back at Mom.

I had always believed Julie would fight for what she wanted but would be fair and ethical when all was said and done. How could she treat our mother that way when she had no more bone marrow and probably only had a year to live? No cloth in the world was worth all that.

I packed it in my bag and noted it was almost exactly the same size as the section of luggage in which it was placed. It zipped in nicely and I returned to my home and put it in my linen cabinet in the dining room. Later, Mother called to tell me that she had neglected to give me the damask napkins that matched the cloth, and I was to pick them up on my next visit home. She told me where she would put them, and that they would be boxed.

About ten days after the tablecloth incident, Julie called me to invite herself, Jim, and Liz, who was near Vickie's age, for a weekend in Illinois. They rarely visited unless Jim had business nearby, or there was a special occasion like Vickie's graduation from high school. I was overjoyed.

Vickie and I had excitedly cleaned the house and prepared the master bedroom for my sister and brother-in-law. I would sleep on the couch and Liz and Vickie would sleep in the two smaller bedrooms, each with a twin bed. Jim and Julie were great people and a lot of fun. After their arrival, the four of us went out for lunch and browsed in the stores downtown. Julie bought some beautiful things for herself and for Christmas. Forever short of money, I bought only the necessary Christmas presents. Jim stayed at the house, doing his paperwork. My sister seemed to thoroughly enjoy her outing. Saturday evening, as we were doing the dishes after dinner, Julie asked casually, "Where is that damask cloth Mother gave you?"

"It's with my linens," I said.

"Could I see it?"

"Why do you want to see it?"

"I just want to see which one it is."

"You saw it when Mother gave it to me."

Julie persisted, "Yes, but I'm just not sure which one it is. Now where do you keep your linens?" She determinedly started into the dining room, staring purposefully at the cabinets. She appeared to be debating which one to open first.

"Why were you so upset with Mother if you don't know what cloth you were upset about?" Julie ignored the question and I followed and showed her the cloth. Julie carefully looked it over. The cloth was still sealed in the laundry package. She did not open it.

"Oh yes, this one." as she handed it back to me to replace in the cabinet.

The rest of the time passed uneventfully, and we all seemed to enjoy ourselves. The only other incident that puzzled me that weekend was early the next morning when, half-awake on the living room couch, I thought I heard something. Getting up and looking around,

I found Julie in her nightgown, leaning up against the kitchen sink in an awkward position, drinking out of a very small glass of water. I asked her what she was doing up at that ungodly hour and she replied she was thirsty. She urged me to return to the couch as she would be going back upstairs in a moment. Several minutes later I heard my sister quietly ascend the stairs, then fell into another deep, pleasant sleep. Sleeping in was a luxury for me as 5:30 was my usual time to get up.

After the holidays, I decided to entertain some friends for dinner to pay back the invitations of the past. I planned the menu and was excited at the thought of how lovely my Wedgewood China would look on such a beautiful cloth. When I removed the cloth from the linen cabinet, I was puzzled. The package appeared smaller than I remembered. When I spread the cloth out on the extended table, it barely covered the top and was of low quality. *How odd*. I couldn't remember Mom ever having a cloth like this. When I packed the cloth, it had been the size and shape of my suitcase. This cloth was considerably smaller. I thought back to the early morning with my sister when she was leaning against the sink in a peculiar way that I now realized was a way to conceal the cloth between herself and the cupboard. Also, for someone who had gotten up at 5:00 am because she was thirsty her glass of water was only four ounces. Painfully, I faced the truth and wondered how to handle it. I took money I really couldn't afford to spend and bought a cloth not nearly as fine as the one my mother had given me. Later, I removed the napkins at the house, confirming what I had so reluctantly wanted to face. In the box my mother had packed were pictures of me as a child and Mom's college papers and diploma. Had Mom packed the diploma and pictures first, then threw in the napkins unthinkingly? I would never know.

Julie had stolen the cloth out of my home. I decided not to say anything. After the grief and shock subsided, I felt sorry for my sister. She must have been inordinately upset to do such a thing. After all, she gave all the Christmas dinners. My final decision was to say nothing until the big family dinners were no longer, then ask for the cloth back, but illness had intervened, and the memory was lost.

I began to recall the details of my last visit to Mother and Dad's, a mere three months before her death. It was for two weeks in August, and she passed away the following November. Mom tried to go through a normal day and somehow succeeded. She and I spent time alone and had long talks. She seemed intent on reviewing designated items and informed me, once again, that my maternal grandfather's 18K gold ring I was to have would be in the safe deposit box, along with my maternal grandmother's gold-filled pendant watch. She offered to get it at that time. "Your Father will take you to the bank while you are here so you can take it." I said I would get it later. She became upset and said, "I'm afraid for you. I'm afraid you won't get it. I believe your sister has other plans. Your Father will take you to the bank now and get what you are to have."

I told Mom I would get it later, insisting "My sister wouldn't do that to me." It was so difficult to accept.

Still believing the cloth incident was an isolated event, I ignored the warning, and added, "You are misjudging her."

"No, I'm not. I have my reasons." I could see she was upset and having trouble coping with whatever was bothering her.

Then, she asked me what things I would like, and I chose the most ornate antique cup and saucer I had ever seen in my years of collecting. She put my name on it. Then I made my choices from my grandmother's treasures and Mom placed my name on the bottoms. I asked about the hand-painted plates, but she didn't seem to feel the urgency about their division and told me to divide them equally with my sister. She called Aunt Beckie to urge her to do the same. Then she asked me if I wanted her Christmas dishes. I said no.

"Julie wants to take them home and, once she gets them there, you may never be able to get them back." Later, Mom told me she had let Julie take the dishes to use but had instructed her to give them to Alison when she passed on. Then, she asked me if I wanted her good dishes. I said I didn't know and again asked why she was asking. It was difficult for me to deal with this and told her to just give me what she wanted me to have. What bothered me was my mother's condition gave her only about a year at the most to live and that year was almost up. Why hadn't she, over the years, designated or disposed of these things? Doing it now only accented the impending death and it was just too painful to deal with. It hadn't occurred to me to urge my parents to put their designations in writing. In hindsight, it might have helped, but given Julie's penchant for stonewalling and manipulations, she probably would have found a way around it. Mom replied, "Julie wants the dishes for Liz. If you want them, I will designate them to you."

"No, Mom, thank you, but I have a nice set. Let her have them." Later I learned Liz had gotten both sets of dishes, unknown to Mother.

Another memory surfaced. Mother and I were sitting at the kitchen table and Dad joined us. He asked Mom if she had told me. I wondered what they were talking about. Mom replied that she hadn't. "Well, you had better tell her," Dad said.

Mom said, "Each time after Julie leaves, there are items missing." She did not elaborate. "I have a great fear that you are going to have trouble with her after we're gone. Julie likes things too much and just insists on having the best of everything and, once she gets them to Williamsport, you may never be able to get them back. We have come to believe that we should designate to you what you are to have now, so there won't be any trouble." I remembered listening quietly but felt that Mom was deteriorating physically, and it was just common sense to assume she was deteriorating mentally as well. They offered no details about the thefts, so that had made it more difficult to accept. At that time, I was torn, vacillating between "my sister wouldn't do that to me" to "if it's really true, how am I supposed to deal with it?" Julie, as far as I knew, was fair and honest, except for that one breach. If this situation really existed, why hadn't my parents been speaking to me about it through the years. Mom had only vaguely alluded to trouble two years prior when we took our trip to Williamsburg. Now, I was able to calculate that was about the time the demitasse spoons disappeared as well as the 24K gold plated comb that sat on the dresser in the guest bedroom, which I had given my mother as a gift.

Mom had looked at Dad, then answered, "I hope I'm wrong, but I don't think I am." She continued with a sigh, "Just remember what I am telling you. There is always one who wants more, thinks they should have it, and will do anything to get it!"

Had my father encouraged my mother to give me the cloth in front of Julie so I could see, firsthand, how my sister acted? Julie had always been argumentative over designations, but far from the behavior she had displayed over the cloth.

My recall included a conversation with my father about why he had wanted to give me the car. "Your Mother and I both wanted this." I knew that my parents, in the last two years of my mother's life, had been critical of Julie and worried about my wellbeing after their deaths. It all became clear and meaningful now and I could pull events together! Now I could remember, *I had told her I didn't want the car if I had to pay for it*! Here was the missing link for me. I *had* Informed her and had not blindly accepted the car without being assured it was free and clear, and then trustingly signed the probate. She had achieved a very successful manipulation because of my fog of illness. The money was extracted surreptitiously, and she added the organ to the probate. This made it clear to me that she knew I was to receive each of those things as gifts so made sure they were on the probate.

Julie had proceeded to steal all designated items, some with my name on them, and all the family memorabilia, refusing to divide any of it. I guess I wasn't even to have my half of the cash from house contents when it would be sold. What Brad had seen in a flash, I was just now pulling together. All I had expected was fairness, a good faith attempt to carry out our parents' and aunt's wishes and the 50-50 terms of the will. I had even offered to divide one-third and two-thirds because I had one daughter and she had two. I began to wonder about my designated jewelry, placed in the safe deposit box for me. When did she pick it up after I revealed where it was? I decided to check it out the next time I was in Michigan. One more thought nagged at me. Had Julie been kind on my first stay at her home because she thought I was going to die, and once she knew I was recovering, she began her assault?

With all of these revelations, I broke into deep sobs. The sister I had known, loved, trusted implicitly, had adamantly defended, had betrayed not only me, but worse, our parents—the ones who had loved her longest. What guided Julie's life? *Oh, what tangled web we weave when first we practice to deceive.* For several days after this, I would break into deep, painful sobs, as if my heart were broken. The sorrow lessened, but there were days when I still had to cope with the grief. I knew that, in spite of that feeling, I would continue to be honest and fair with her.

FIFTEEN

ACCOUNTABILITY

1992

Would I ever know the answers to all the new insights, questions, and suspicions? Probably not. Julie had avoided accountability of Dad's finances all along. When Brad came home, I discussed her lack of transparency and gave an example.

Dad had developed emphysema since Mom's death as he had returned to smoking. As a result, the window air conditioners had to be on at all times. My utility bills skyrocketed. In tears, I called Julie, appalled at the size of my electric bill. When Julie heard my dilemma, she said she would send me $800, and it didn't have to be paid back. In retrospect now, and connecting actions with more clarity, did Julie take $800 for herself as well from Dad's checking account, instead of seeing the cost as extra living expenses? Or she may have simply deducted it from my inheritance as the cash was distributed.

I could remember that there had been a toilet that became plugged, the one Dad used all the time. He jumped in and paid cash for the plumber. When Julie found out, she had angrily demanded, "How much did he pay out for you?" In retrospect, had Julie extracted a like amount from Dad's checking account for herself instead of considering this money as an extra expense of Dad's? Julie informed me that there was money to help us if Dad would just cash his money markets. She said that he refused to do so and asked me to intervene. I promised I would speak to him.

When I approached Dad about money markets and told him Julie was urging that they be cashed in, he answered, "I want that money accounted for after I'm gone, and if I cash the money markets now, I can't be sure that will be done or how the money will be divided." He seemed fearful and hesitant. Why had Dad given my sister Power of Attorney if he didn't trust her? My parents believed Julie was stealing out of the house but gave her Power of Attorney? I tried to calm his fears, ignorant of Julie's plots. My thought was that he must trust Julie and Jim as they were looking out for his best interests. Finally, Dad reluctantly agreed to cash in the money markets. That fall, the first check arrived. Julie had sent my part of a check but no documentation with it, nor was there ever any with any of the checks she sent. I began to wonder if I had made another colossal mistake in my life by not moving back to the hometown after my second divorce. Things would probably have been much different where Julie was concerned. I loved my job and it had great benefits, and I hated to give up friendships, hated to pull Vickie out of school and away from her friends and skating under Della to whom she had grown so close. I wanted her to have her weekends with her father. Of course, at the time, I didn't discuss it with Brad as it never occurred to me.

When I discussed this with Brad, he said he didn't think Julie would have acted any differently except by my being there, she might have had to be more transparent about the money. He went home to Michigan every three weeks after our divorce, so he would have been able to spend time with Vickie and I would have been able to spend time with my parents. For a long time after our conversation, I felt a deep regret I had not done things differently.

There was another element to all of

this: without the floods and stress, would I be a well person today?

*   *   *   *   *

A few days after Brad's and my discussion, Julie called and told me that there was a bill before the state legislature that would take the houses of those in long term care when the cash was gone. "At the rate the money is being used for Aunt Beckie's long-term care, that will be in December," Julie informed me, "so you may get the key from Faith and take what you want because it will all be gone by the end of the year."

Brad had told me this very thing the night before as Julie had called him at his office, but it had been hard for me to believe. This didn't sound like the Julie I had come to know. She probably meant that anything left after she had taken what she wanted, I could have.

Brad said, "It will mean doing an inventory, so everything is accounted for. This will be joint property." *An inventory?* There hadn't been one done at my parents' home. Maybe Julie was going to at least divide Aunt Beckie's cherished and valuable items with me. A few weeks later, Brad called his nephews, who lived within fifty miles of our hometown, and made arrangements for them to come a few days early before hunting season started. "They have pick-up trucks," Brad reasoned, "and it will make the move go faster."

We left the following week and Vickie accompanied us. On arriving at the house, we found dog poop in my old bedroom, next to David's bed. We cleaned it up but were appalled at Julie's attempt to keep Vickie from bringing her dog to the house when Elizabeth obviously had a dog too.

On this trip, I was able to sleep in Mom's bed. I was ecstatic. The following morning, I awoke to see Laurie, my roommate from nurses' training, who had arrived to spend a week with Brad and me. We rarely got to see each other, and this would be twice in one year. She was a cheerful, sturdy, and sparkling girl who knew how to do everything. She was a wonderful seamstress and, as her girls grew up, she made them and herself many of their own clothes, refinished furniture, was a terrific cook, and baked effortlessly. Also, she canned a lot of the family's food. Brad referred to her as a typical farm girl.

The morning of her arrival, Laurie was determined to get breakfast for everyone. Mornings were difficult for me. The slow riser in me since the onset of my illness was in great contrast to Laurie, who was absolutely radiant in the morning. She came into the bedroom to ask where the frying pans were as she was unable to find them. I told her to look on the shelves under the stove. Laurie replied that she had looked there. Together we went through every item under the stove and the other cupboards. Then, we moved to the summer kitchen and carefully looked over every item there. No frying pans. No pans of any kind. My mother's good stainless steel Revere ware was gone. There was only an old, flat pan Mom had used to make pancakes years ago, which was hanging from a nail on the wall in the summer kitchen. Laurie cooked breakfast on the old, flat pan. Later, Brad brought pans in from the family farm to use during our stay.

After breakfast, Laurie went with Brad, Vickie, and me to Aunt Beckie's house after picking up the key from Faith. She informed me that Julie had the idea I only wanted a music stand. "You loved your aunt and lived with her. Don't you want more than that?" No wonder Julie had appeared so generous. Brad clearly explained that an inventory was needed, and probate protocol would be followed. We explained our decision to Faith.

We looked around and Laurie began to point out antiques and collectibles in the house that were of value. I did not have much interest in antiques, sentimental pieces were more meaningful to me. Faith followed us over to the house to show me the condition of the antique furniture. These pieces had been sitting in the house for so long with the heat turned low that there was mildew on a lot of the surfaces. Some pieces were actually wet.

Laurie informed me that eventually it would ruin the finish. The three of us talked over the manpower available to move these things to my parents' home. Faith urged us to do so. I was spurred on by the knowledge that the State might take all of this by the end of the year, or maybe Julie intended to take all of it. I still wasn't sure, but since I had been repeatedly chastised for not doing any work at the house, here was my chance to contribute something.

Brad's nephews arrived and the antique furniture was cleaned and moved. The antique, seven-foot black walnut mirror was carefully carried to the truck, where the nephews had placed a mattress in the bed of the truck solely for the purpose of transporting the mirror. With Laurie's help, we began to transfer the contents of drawers and my aunt's curio cabinet and shelves to boxes to be transported. Laurie tirelessly helped and even did some deep cleaning at my parents' house, which needed it badly. Apparently, Julie and her family only cleaned superficially, even though they used the house a lot. She also informed me that doilies needed to be kept on Mom's and Dad's beautiful bedroom set because old finishes were fragile. We set about trying to locate linens, as I could remember Mom had kept doilies on her dressers, but all had been removed. We found the long-forgotten linens and covered the flat surfaces of the dressers.

I began to wrap and pack the antique pieces from my aunt's China cabinet into boxes. My grandmother, at one time, had a China cabinet to die for. There was Nippon, Roseville pottery, German pieces, and the beautiful and coveted hand-painted plates with roses. My thoughts turned to my mother and Aunt Beckie. They had their differences through the years but managed to divide their parents' estate evenly, each sister taking two very ornate Victorian cups and saucers, half of the antique Victorian plates, and each had half of the family jewelry. Aunt Beckie had all the antique family pictures, historical papers and furniture, but only because Abbie disliked "old stuff", as she called it. My desperate wish was that Julie and I could do this as well. The prospects did not look good for that kind of outcome. Since our grandmother's cherished items were all gone somewhere, being "protected," maybe Julie would be willing to divide what was left of these things in a fair manner. Especially since we were doing all the work to save them.

Upon packing, I noticed there were four cups and saucers, one mine and three of my mother's, hanging in the cabinet where my aunt's missing beautiful antique cups and saucers had hung, as well as a plain Nippon cup and saucer and a paper-thin, beautiful oriental cup. It had been understood that each girl was to receive two of the ornate cups and saucers. The two at my parents' place still hung in the kitchen, with each daughter's name on them. I assumed Julie wouldn't touch anything that was obviously in plain view. The question was, how had my mother's cups and mine gotten here? Julie, of course. Where were the other antique cups and saucers they had replaced? If my mother was right, they were in Williamsport, *"Once she gets them there..."*

I would have to look more carefully at my mother's cup collection to make sure Julie hadn't brought them to the house. I looked but never found the two antique cups and saucers of Aunt Beckie's among my mother's. The plainer, Nippon cup and saucer missing from Aunt Beckie's was found hidden in the back of a kitchen cabinet at my family home, and the beautiful oriental cup was gone.

There were a lot of Victorian pictures and small portraits from the 1800s through the mid-1920s and even two portraits of my mother I had never seen before, probably the most beautiful pictures of her I had ever seen. Fortunately, there were two. Even though all had been designated to me, I was sure Julie would want one of these. In looking through all of them, I noticed some were missing. I filled three large drawers at my parents' place. They would be shared with Julie. There were many identical portraits and enough to easily go around. My plan for family albums included family histories. Maybe Julie would like me to do an album for her. Would she be willing to return what she had taken as a kind, reciprocal gesture? Would she share the pictures she removed from the house?

We packed the Victorian, hand-painted rose plates. Among them was a plate, my favorite, that had been missing from mother's China cabinet long before the entire contents disappeared. Where was my aunt's plate that my mother's plate had replaced? Julie knew that Faith counted and kept track of Aunt Beckie's eighteen plates and everything else in the house and occasionally wrote things down so she could be accurate in reporting to the family. It would seem Julie had tried to keep the count at eighteen when she extracted the one she wanted. The plate count was eighteen in the cabinet, five hanging on the walls, and five on the shelves in the dining room and living room that were probably inherited by Aunt Beckie from her father-in-law as they were different from my grandmother's. Since Mom's were gone, at least Aunt Beckie's were mostly intact.

Aunt Beckie had a lot of silver, two full sets, and extra dessert forks which were carefully put away at my family home. Also, there were two valuable items, a leather pouch full of gold dust and a rose gold brooch that had our maternal grandmother's maiden initial engraved on it. They were carefully locked in my aunt's desk that had been moved into Mom's upstairs storeroom at the house.

Aunt Beckie's two plain oil lamps were washed and placed in the back storeroom cupboard and the ornate one was placed at the very back of the highest shelf in the summer kitchen. I had noticed Mom's most ornate oil lamp was missing. This one would probably disappear too. At least Julie would have to look very hard for it in order to steal it. Why couldn't she ask me if she could have it? Why was she so unable to be open and honest about her actions, especially since I probably would have agreed?

Vickie saw items she liked and wanted. That wasn't what one does in an estate division, it was explained. Nothing, especially those items of value, should be touched because it was joint property until the heirs get together to identify what they wanted and tossed a coin for any items they might both want. There was a sheet of music that I had lost in the two floods and was happy to see that my aunt also had my favorite piece. I knew Julie wasn't interested in the music, and I would inform her. I let Vickie take a broken frog doorstop from the basement so she could restore it in her art class. Julie would be informed as well.

Laurie offered to take the down pillows, wash and recover them. I accepted her offer immediately. She took a homemade quilt that needed repair as well and brought it back, looking new, to be sold at the estate sale.

In an old brown paper bag in the

back bedroom, I found a piece of my grandmother's Victorian satin brocade curtain that was badly shredded, but there was a four by five swatch of cloth still in good shape. Faith was there and told me Julie had removed Aunt Beckie's large tablecloth of the same material as soon as my aunt was placed in long term care. Laurie offered to make a small tablecloth for me, and I happily consented. As the moving progressed, Faith wondered if I was going to take Aunt Beckie's bed. Her question made me wonder if she had heard about the bed problem at the house, "No, why?"

"Because it is a wonderful and expensive bed your mother bought for Beckie because of her rheumatoid arthritis." It was just another example to me of how Abbie and Beckie, despite their bickering, were good to one another.

There were Victorian Christmas ornaments, Victorian Christmas cards given and received. These were saved. I still hoped Julie would relent and bring back all the "protected" items. Brad adamantly told me I should plan to never see them again.

There was a flurry of activity over five days. There proved to be so much to move that time was running out and we hadn't finished. The inventory was done, but I was not feeling well by the end of the five days and knew it wasn't as complete or detailed as it should have been. Never having done an inventory before, the effort was a conscientious one but lacking in the knowledge needed to do a proper, more detailed one. Fortunately, I took the inventory with me when we left to return to Illinois.

We visited Aunt Beckie several times during the week. On our last visit to the long-term care facility, we stopped at the bank to check my parents' safe deposit box, where my designated items had been placed for me. I could remember that, after informing Julie where these things should be, she insisted they were missing, then had said that there was nothing in writing and had kept my designated jewelry. When had Julie gone to the safe deposit box?

I entered the bank and approached the assistant bank manager, whom I had known since childhood. After exchanging pleasantries, I asked to see the record of entries into my parents' safe deposit box. Allie was hesitant, and my thought for a moment was that she would refuse. There was a long pause, then she said, "I don't know if can let you see these records."

"Probate is over, and I would very much like to see the signed entry card."

She paused a moment longer, got up from her desk, and went to a file cabinet. She extracted a card and handed it to me. The last date on the card was just before New Year's, written by Julie after I had left for Illinois for my appointment with the hematologist. I silently berated myself for not connecting Jim's and Julie's quick trip home during terrible weather when I wasn't there. This revelation was a stunning blow, the stark realization of the lengths Julie would go to carry out her plots.

Arriving at long-term care, I noted that Aunt Beckie had failed terribly since Fourth of July, when we had last visited. I couldn't help but feel her days were numbered. She was nearly ninety-two and often said," I can't hear well, and I can't see much. I don't know why the good Lord lets me live," but was still able to hold my hands and say, "We have always had such a great love for each other." Aunt Beckie, even now, still complained about the $4000 that had never been put in her bank account. I asked if there was some error as Jim was a millionaire and Julie certainly shouldn't need to steal $4000, but Aunt Beckie was adamant.

I had once again brought her a box of chocolates and told her we were leaving.

Brad was waiting in the car. Aunt Beckie hugged me as if she would never let me go. "Oh, just let me hold you a moment longer." I felt a deep loss as I left my aunt that day. Being physically unable to care for her was painful for me, and I felt sure I would not see her alive again.

We left after assuring Faith we would inform my sister of the removal of the contents of Aunt Beckie's house. There were still some things to be sorted out and brought to the parental home, but that would be mentioned to Julie. Perhaps she would finish the job. We had done our part to save the contents from the wrecking ball.

The ride to Illinois was a blur. Exhausted, I slept most of the way lying in the backseat. Vickie survived the week better than I had. Brad and I dropped her off and went home.

*   *   *   *   *

When we arrived back at Brad's apartment, I didn't feel my best, but there was a feeling of pride at how well I had held up. Several days later, I called Julie. It was a late Wednesday afternoon. My sister bowled on Wednesday afternoons with the girls. When she answered, her speech sounded slightly slurred.

"You don't have to worry about the State taking Aunt Beckie's contents," I said. "Most of it is moved to our place. We had a lot of strong bodies, the weather was wonderful, and it just seemed the right thing to do. We did this for both our sakes. However, there are still things to be moved, so when you are there next, maybe you could finish up."

"Oh yeah?" Julie replied in a nasty tone, which shocked me. I had felt optimistic calling her to tell her this and thought she would be relieved—maybe even pleased.

In an earlier phone call, I had related to Sharon how hard we all worked during Brad's vacation week and Sharon had sounded so pleased: "How nice of you to do all that work and save the property."

Ignoring Julie's negative attitude, I continued, "There are a lot of antique portraits we should go over together and make choices."

"Where were they?! Where did you find them?" Julie spat out in a rage. She sounded positively hateful. I could picture her face contorted in anger. When she slurred, you knew you were in for it.

"In Aunt Beckie's back bedroom," I answered, trying to keep my voice benign. The thought occurred to me that Julie must have been looking for pictures, had already removed some to Williamsport from the parental home. I did not remind Julie that the portraits had been promised to me, because I had always intended to divide them with my sister if she wished. They had been left at Aunt Beckie's for that very reason. *She's probably in a rage because she missed a few...* How unbelievable!

"What about the silver?" she shouted. "Faith says you have a chest full of silver!"

"The only silver we have is what Aunt Beckie gave Vickie, which I showed you some years ago. There was no chest."

"Well, Faith was there, and you certainly did take a chest full of silver when you moved that stuff!" The psych nurse in me kicked in and I grabbed a pen and paper and took it all down in shorthand, determined to have an accurate account of the bizarre exchange.

"Julie, I have no chest," I replied.

"YES, YOU DO!! THE SILVER was in a CHEST, and YOU HAVE IT!!"

"I am telling you I don't. The silver is wrapped in a cloth," I answered firmly, struggling to remain unintimidated.

Julie was screaming into the phone: "NO, IT ISN'T!!! FAITH SAID YOU HAVE A CHEST FULL OF SILVER!!!"

"I don't have a chest full of silver."

"YES, YOU DO!" She was screaming so

loud her voice began to crack.

"No, I don't."

"YES, YOU DO!!"

I had heard enough. "I don't CARE what Faith said, she's wrong!" I continued in a calmer voice: "Vickie's silver was wrapped in a sort of felt cloth. This is all the silver we have."

"Well, where is the chest then?" Julie sounded more in control but still tight with anger.

"I think the chest you may be referring to might be on a table next to the couch in Aunt Beckie's dining room. There was nothing in it. Bring it over with the other things that still need to come."

"No, I won't," Julie retorted. "That chest was promised to Alison." I wanted to ask if there was anything in writing but withheld the comment.

"And we should keep dollies and linens on Mother's and Dad's bedroom set as Laurie says old finishes are fragile and to keep them protected."

Julie replied in a hateful voice, "Who is this person?!"

I didn't answer because, if Julie thought about it, she did know who Laurie was. I went on to explain we had found linens, and all was taken care of, then asked where Mother's frying pans and her other Revere ware was.

"Well, they're there!"

"All of the stainless-steel pans are gone."

"They're there," she repeated. "You just didn't look."

"We looked around thoroughly."

"Well, I don't *have* them!" I carried it no further. My sister was a master at evasion and would argue forever. I had to conclude Julie must have given the pans to one of her girls, or she took them with her each time she left due to her unfounded fear I was stealing from the house. Who knew? I had noted that there was also something missing from the attic. Later, I was able to recall it was a doll house and remembered Mom had told me it wasn't the one I had as a child and that Julie wanted it.

I suggested to Julie that we have Faith do a thorough fall cleaning at our parents' place. "The house really needs it."

"You never cared before!" Julie shot back.

Why couldn't she understand that with improvement in my condition I was noticing more of the world around me? "The house is dirty, let's get it cleaned. The window wells are filthy, the rug in Dad's and Mother's bedroom needs shampooing. Laurie cleaned the big front window because it looked grimy. Vickie took it upon herself to clean the stove. She wore rubber gloves and it's sparkling now." I didn't tell Julie that the stove was Vickie's favorite thing. It was a high-end stove, and she loved the chrome ovens and all the lights. She did complain, however, that it was so filthy, it looked as though no one had touched the ovens, the lights, or under the hot plates since her grandmother had passed away."

I had not been able to find my favorite childhood doll that Mom had kept for me, as well as my porcelain play dishes from childhood that were now considered collectables. I had searched everywhere for them to no avail, so I asked about them.

Julie huffed. "Well, I don't know." I told my sister goodbye and hung up with a sigh of relief but also hurt feelings at my sister's inability or unwillingness to understand how limited I had been during most of my illness.

Despite these difficulties with my sister, I was still determined to go through with an attempt to show Julie what fairness was in estate division. It seemed she had no concept. The encounter, particularly the accusations about the silver, upset me. There was now a record, word for word, of what Julie had spewed forth. I typed it and wrote Julie a letter with the descriptive encounter included. "I couldn't believe what I was hearing. Who are you? Who have you become? Please take a long look at yourself."

Several days later, Alison called. She said she didn't understand why I had moved things without telling her mother. The whole family would have come to help.

"I understand your feelings and concerns for your mother," I replied, "but we thought we were doing a good thing and never meant to offend anyone."

Alison replied, "I'm just trying to keep the lines of communication open. I don't want this family to break up." Had Julie shown her my letter? Most likely not. That was the part she kept hidden. Absorbing my sister's venom, I began to worry about something done unthinkingly as we moved contents from Aunt Beckie's to my parents' home. The brocade cloth Laurie had made for me had been placed on the Victorian library table brought over from Aunt Beckie's. It needed refinishing, so to make it look decent we placed the cloth over it. My fear was that Julie would even take that if she had the chance. I called Faith and told her. She would get it for me and place a different cloth on that table.

A week or two later, Faith called all

upset. Unbeknownst to us both, Julie had told the next-door neighbor to let her know immediately if anyone entered the house. Only two other people besides her family had a key. What paranoia! There had never been a break-in of anyone's home in our small town.

Julie went to Faith's home and confronted her, told her she was the Representative and whatever Faith removed from the house for me was to be handed over to her. Faith admitted she had done something she shouldn't have done. She meekly handed the cloth over to Julie. The very thing I didn't want to happen, happened! Unsure of what my next move would be, I spent the next couple of weeks in contemplation of a future action. My response would come sooner than anticipated.

*   *   *   *   *

Three weeks later, Julie called and gently informed me that Aunt Beckie had passed away. "You won't be coming, will you, since you were just here?"

"Yes, absolutely, we will be coming."

"You were just here," she repeated, sounding annoyed.

"Doesn't matter, we are coming anyway. She was my other mother, and you know that!" Tears began streaming down my cheeks.

Julie sounded less than pleased, then proceeded to give me the rushed funeral plans. We would really have to scramble to be there for the funeral, but with any luck at all we might make the final evening of visitation. I asked what all the rush was about. She mumbled something about the funeral director only having one opening. The funeral home serviced Bay Harbor and the surrounding area, which was probably not more than 2800 people. The funeral home was large, with three rooms for services that could be divided in half if the family was small. I had never known this funeral director to force early funerals. In my opinion, this was one more tactic to exclude me from the family. Why hadn't I been informed before the funeral arrangements were made so I could be present the first night of visitation? Hanging up, I sobbed for the loss of Aunt Beckie and the last of my loving and supportive family.

SIXTEEN

JULIE REVEALS HERSELF

1992

For the second time in three weeks, Brad made a bed for me in the backseat of the car. We made arrangements to pick up Vickie on the way. Arriving near midnight, Jim, Julie, and the girls and their families were at the house, and we went on to the farm. The first night of the visitation had taken place, and there was only one more day at the funeral home in which Julie and I would have to greet visitors. The funeral would be held in the church where Aunt Beckie had given so much of herself.

The next afternoon, when Brad, Vickie, and I arrived at the funeral home, neither Julie nor her family were there yet. They came in about a half hour later. Julie appeared stiff and seemed to be seething with anger. There were moments when hostility seemed to fairly spill over in her facial expressions. Brad's words came back to me "Your sister can't stand it that you are being assertive. She's paranoid and judges you by her own behavior."

Jim and the girls seemed their usual selves, only they seemed subdued when they greeted me. Julie approached me without a greeting. Whispering angrily, she said, "You know, you turned off the light switch that controls the sump pump in Aunt Beckie's basement when you were there, and her basement was flooded. Jason, Faith's husband, had to crawl into the basement through the window and wade through deep water. If there is any damage, it is YOUR FAULT!" A look of pure hatred was etched across her face.

I kept my tone even as I spoke, "You will have to speak to Brad about whatever he did or did not do. I was never in the basement."

Julie walked away and never mentioned the incident to Brad.

Later that day, she once again approached me with a booklet that contained Xeroxed copies of some of the antique portraits in our family's collection. "Have you seen this booklet before?" she asked.

"No. Where did you get it?"

"I got it from Ardis Brown, as she had borrowed our pictures for an article she was writing about the hometown residents. I went to her and got it. Do you know where these pictures are?"

"Yes. They are in with the pictures I brought over from Aunt Beckie's. There are three large drawers full that she gave me"—I didn't mention that there were some missing— "but I thought we should go through them *together*." I had always felt there was a special place in hell for people who didn't share pictures.

People streamed in all afternoon and evening. Aunt Beckie hadn't been forgotten in all the years she had been retired, and old students remembered their favorite teacher and came back to bid their final farewells, some in tears.

The funeral was held the following afternoon. It was a clear and sunny day as Aunt Beckie's soul entered the pearly gates she had been longing for. We stood in the church yard as the casket was loaded into the hearse and Jenny Barker, a longtime friend of the family and a very close friend of Aunt Beckie's, came up to me. "You are looking good. My, you've made marvelous improvement, haven't you?"

"Yes," I smilingly replied, "but I am a little tired. Two trips within three weeks is a little too demanding."

"Well, it is so wonderful to see you

looking so well. I will never forget the day your sister called me and told me you had what your mother had and were going to die. Although I have never had a chance to know you as well as Julie, I certainly feel connected because of my close relationship with your family, and especially your Aunt Beckie. I am so happy for you."

Did Julie think she was going to be the only heir if she could just stall long enough, or was I being too cynical? This new revelation took my breath away.

Before I could start for the car, Faith caught up with me, squeezed my arm, murmured her condolences, then asked what happened that I couldn't be at the first night of visitation. "The room was packed with relatives and friends who wondered why you weren't there."

I answered, "Julie made all the arrangements without consulting me. We couldn't make it any sooner."

We parted, with Faith inviting me to her home before we left if we had time. Brad, Vickie, and I went to the cemetery. I was touched that Faith was attempting to befriend me. I really didn't know her very well. My impression was that she knew more than she would openly speak about and was maybe even disillusioned over Julie's behavior.

There was a luncheon at the church following the burial, but the two families sat apart without speaking.

A former student of Aunt Beckie's had become a journalist and wrote about her in the paper. Faith would later send me a copy:

A former schoolteacher of mine, Rebecca Ellsworth, died this week. She was 91.

Mrs. Ellsworth was a crusty, feisty, fun-loving blast of energy. She could pound a piano hard enough to make it groan. One of the things she thought important for youngsters to learn was poetry. I remember a poem she made us memorize, a fragment of which is:

It's just a little thing to do.

Just to think.

Anyone, no matter who,

Ought to think

So take a little time each day,

Take it from your work or play

But: Stop and think.

Here's thinking of you, Mrs. Ellsworth.

*　　*　　*　　*　　*

The following day, we prepared to depart once more for Illinois. I had assured Julie I would pick up the cards from mourners from the funeral home and help write thank-you notes. The car packed, we set out for my parents' place. Brad was adamant he had to be back to work the following day. I would have liked to have stayed and get my designated items as well as force division of my pictures, our grandmother's porcelain Victorian plates, and other pieces. I realized with the time constraints this was not going to be possible. Now would have been such a good time, since Jim was there to hear what had really been going on.

As we pulled into the yard, Liz and her family were packing their van and Jim was helping them. Brad, Vickie, and I exited our car and, as we were about to enter the house, Jim stopped to comment, "You folks really did a lot of work." It sounded as though it was a compliment.

Brad and I smilingly agreed that it had been. We had spent a week of Brad's vacation time trying to save the contents from the State's wrecking ball.

When we entered the kitchen from the back door, Julie was standing there, scowling. She gave me the cards I had come to pick up and asked when we were leaving.

"We're on our way," I answered. "When I come back in the spring, we should get together and go through all of these things and divide. And, by the way, I found four cups and saucers of Mother's at Aunt Beckie's when we moved the curio cabinet contents." My intent was to gently impress upon her that I was more alert, and she needed to be accountable. I added that one of our grandmother's Victorian plates that was Mother's was found with Aunt Beckie's. "How did they get there?" I asked.

My sister shrugged. "I don't know. Mother must have taken them over there."

I knew Julie was not telling the truth as the cup and saucer that were mine had been in my up-stairs bedroom and only after Dad died had I brought them downstairs. Mother's plate had been in her China cabinet until those contents disappeared. Gently, I dared to remind her of that.

Julie sniffed. "You're wrong!"

Apparently, she didn't intend to be truthful and would never explain or apologize for her behavior. I loved the antique cups and saucers and had been collecting them since I was sixteen. Julie had never been interested until now. I did not pursue the matter further. To confront

Julie too hard over these matters would be like waving a red flag in front of a bull.

Julie, not to be outdone and believing that the best defense is a great offense, started in on me. "By the way," she pointed out crossly, "here are the pans you said weren't here. They were here all the time! You just didn't see them!" She led me into the summer kitchen and showed me Mother's stainless-steel pans hanging under the pancake pan Laurie had used.

"They weren't here. We looked."

"They were here! They were hanging right here all the time!" Julie looked down her nose at me disapprovingly.

I looked my sister in the eye, shook my head slowly 'no', and turned away, walking back into the kitchen.

Matter-of-factly, I asked where Mom's ornate oil lamp was. "There should have been three," I reminded Julie.

"There weren't three. Mother didn't have three," Julie announced, once again ready to argue into oblivion.

"Mother and Aunt Beckie each had three…"

"Well, I don't know where it is. I don't have it!" Julie replied stubbornly.

At that moment, Jim and Liz entered the kitchen, still packing the van. Their presence gave Julie the audience she needed to try and make me look bad. She exploded, suddenly consumed with anger and strutting around the kitchen. "And what did you take?"

"I have a piece of music, a piece I lost in the flood, that is all. I knew you wouldn't want it." I paused and added, "You'll have to excuse me. I guess I forgot to tell you when I called you."

Julie moved menacingly toward me and shook her finger within an inch of my nose, "You better not touch *anything* here! We are going to videotape everything!"

I kept my voice low. "Julie, what's wrong with you? Why are you acting this way?"

Jim jumped in to defend Julie. "You do ask an awful lot of questions."

I felt like telling him I had a right to ask as many questions as I pleased, but I didn't want to sound defiant. Struggling to remain calm, I turned to my brother-in-law: "Jim, we have a lot of stuff here, with some missing, and we better damn well know or find out where things are. "

"I want the key to the desk!" Julie shouted. "Give it to me!"

I calmly mocked my sister. "I don't *have* it!" In reality, Julie didn't need a key and I was sure she knew that. Everything in the house was accessible to her. She just wanted to assert her authority. All she needed to get into the desk was a paperclip.

"I want to know what you've taken!" she demanded.

"I haven't taken anything and, while we are on this subject, you went over to Faith's and told her you were the Representative, and she was to give you whatever it was she removed from the house for me. Apparently, you had our neighbor report to you if anyone came into the house. Who reports to me when you enter the house and remove contents that is joint property? "Leave my things alone—and you aren't the Representative any longer in Dad's estate."

"Faith must have misunderstood because I didn't say that."

"Everyone always 'misunderstands' you, Julie. Don't you think that is rather strange? If you can have a brocade cloth, so can I, so please return it. Now, I'd like to talk about the gun…"

"What about it?" she asked.

"Where is it?"

"I don't know. I don't have it!"

"Brad should have been presented with the gun, Julie. It was designated to him." Brad stood silently beside me.

"I don't know where it is. I don't know anything about the gun." She turned to Jim and winked. Brad and I both saw it and looked at each other knowingly.

"Well, I have talked this over with Brad and he says to give the gun to Jim. Jim is the son-in-law and Brad says he can have the gun. He told Mother this when she insisted that she wanted him to have it."

Julie and Jim exchanged glances before my sister put her hands in the pockets of her slacks, looked down at the floor, and walked away. She clearly was not expecting this act of generosity. Then, she walked back over to her husband and winked again, asking if he knew anything about the gun. Jim began to laugh, reminiscent of the time he had laughed so hard when Julie was trying to get me to agree to a joint deed for the parental home. Jim turned to me and asked if I remembered he was to have the grill and Brad the gun and explained that the gun was in Williamsport. He asserted, "Lee gave it to me for safe keeping, but Julie didn't know it was there." Jim to the rescue!

I wasn't fooled. There wasn't anything in Julie's house that she didn't know was there. Secondly, Dad had never given them the gun. He had complained Julie was removing items from the house. It was just another designated item that she intended to keep. If her family backed up her lies, there wasn't much hope of any fairness toward me. This act of generosity toward them had enlisted some kind of reaction in Julie, but I doubted that would change her overall plan to take the best of everything from both estates. I started having second thoughts about my pictures, but it was too late to haul three large drawers out to a crowded car.

Then I related as benignly as possible that Vickie and I had found dog poop next to David's bed. Both Jim and Julie glared at me with no comment. I quickly added, "I'm not trying to make an issue of this. I'm just trying to make you aware so the dog can be watched more closely."

Then, Julie asked politely where Aunt Beckie's beautiful oil lamp was. I was tired and slow to recall. I told her they were all in the cupboard in the back storeroom off the kitchen. She replied that there were only two and asked where the third one was. I said that we had moved so much of my aunt's property I couldn't remember. To my surprise, she seemed to accept this quietly. This was the sister I used to know.

As we left, I said, "When I come back, let's go through the pictures and everything together."

Julie made no comment. *Should I stay and force her to divide right now?* I had no car and couldn't yet shop for myself so reluctantly I put the thought away.

Brad and I left, stopping briefly at Faith's to say goodbye and promising to spend time with her on our next visit. On the way to Illinois, Brad and I discussed what had just happened. Brad concluded we had just witnessed a "Dungeons and Dragons" player in action. "She will carry things as far as she can and will always carry it farther than the other person. Your sister has quite an arsenal of bad behavior. It will be interesting to see what she does next."

I mimicked my sister: "What did you take?" And "Don't you dare use the house. If I was going to steal anything, wouldn't I have done it before this? She really put on a show. I just want division. Let's plan for spring," I told Brad, "since you have to get back to work." Exhausted, I put my head down on my pillow and slept most of the way back.

*   *   *   *   *

A week later, I sat down to write my sister but wondered if I should tell her where Aunt Beckie's beautiful oil lamp was. If I did, I suspected it would be gone on my return. I had simply been too tired and truly couldn't remember where I had placed it. Maybe telling her would inspire her to respond in kind. That hope was balanced by another opposite and strong possibility: that Julie viewed joint property as mostly hers alone. Alison's words came back to me, "My mother is always right, she is never wrong, and she never apologizes." I wrote the letter anyway and hoped for a positive reaction.

Several weeks later, I received a letter from my sister. She made accusations about the oil lamp, changing the facts and accusing me of insisting there were two lamps. She even insisted her family had heard me say this! Julie went on to state that the "lamp scenario is indicative of a more serious problem that has happened consistently."

I couldn't believe what was an obvious attempt to discredit anything I might ask about or say to her. I felt this idea might have come from an incident at the church luncheon following Aunt Beckie's burial. We had all been seated at a long table, eating. I was sitting with a first cousin and his wife. Julie, Liz, and Jim had been sitting at the next table, and Julie and her daughter seemed to be straining to hear what we were talking about. They asked what my illness was like. I told them how, when I was very ill, I wasn't very good at remembering how to balance my checkbook and had to rely on the statement directions. I saw Liz whisper something in her mother's ear.

In her letter, Julie went on to say, "Our relationship has now been destroyed by judgments, suspicions, accusations, and inaccuracies and it would be a total act of dishonesty for us to continue contact." Julie added, "The only thing remaining between us is the business of the two houses." She ended the letter with the hope I would be able to maintain a business-like attitude in the future.

I was aghast! Who had been business-like? If Julie was so business-like, why hadn't she followed probate protocol instead of manipulating the process to her own benefit? And what about the hissy fits? Was that business-like? There seemed no end to her obfuscations.

*　　*　　*　　*　　*

After the holidays, I wrote to Julie, asking her what she saw as my role in the estate matters. I asked that we hold a division by spring so all would be finished. The letter ended with, "We seem to have a conflict between our individual philosophies of life."

Within a few days, Julie called in a fury

and spat out loudly over the phone: "GET OUT OF MY LIFE! STAY OUT OF MY LIFE! I DON'T WANT TO HEAR FROM YOU, SPEAK TO YOU, OR HAVE TO LOOK AT YOU!"

"Why are you insistent on this, Julie? Why can't there be some give and take in the issues I have raised?"

"Because you don't care about me or my family!" The receiver clicked.

The winter passed with no more communication between us. There had been a letter from an attorney, who was going to probate Aunt Beckie's estate, asking me to sign the forms, as Julie had asked to be Representative. I studied the forms, discussed my feelings with Brad. I decided to call the attorney before signing anything. The next afternoon, I placed a call to him.

I identified myself and stated I was having difficulty with signing the papers he had sent. The probate attorney seemed ill at ease as I spoke about the situation between myself and my sister. Consequently, I told him I would be uncomfortable about Julie being involved in another probate, as our parents' Will had not been properly executed. The attorney cut me off as I began to give specific instances and asked me why he should believe me. I said, "Because I am telling you the truth. I am being completely open and honest with you."

Now he sounded not only uncomfortable but annoyed. However, he did state that Aunt Beckie's estate was a small one and not much was involved. He asked me to please sign and return the papers.

When Brad arrived home from work that day, I discussed the situation with him. He assured me that Chris Donovan was a very reputable attorney, following in his father's footsteps. He urged me to sign the papers but to put in writing my concerns.

The next day, I sat down and composed a letter with an apology for causing him any discomfort. I requested he keep the information disclosed confidential and use it only when and how he felt it should be used. I reiterated in so many words that there was never a final accounting of the money from our father's estate. The letter ran two pages and I hoped he would take the time to read it. I signed the necessary probate papers and Brad mailed the letter and forms the next day. The letter was marked "Confidential."

* * * * *

In April, I wrote Julie a letter to inform

her when we would be coming to Michigan in May. I did not respond to her latest accusations in her last letter. Once again, I requested my designated jewelry and other items. "I am grateful you could be there for Mom and Dad when I couldn't. You were the one that was there, and I want you to know how much I appreciate that. Hopefully we can get together and make choices."

I had chosen this time in May because it was the time of year when Julie monopolized the house. I was hopeful that, this time, things would go more smoothly, and Julie would be on her best behavior. I was not ready to give up on my sister.

SEVENTEEN

JULIE TAKES CONTROL

1993

May came, and despite hearing nothing from Julie, Brad and I once again returned to the hometown but stayed at the family farm. The day after our arrival, we went to my parents' place, expecting Julie and Jim to be there. The house was vacant.

I contacted the probate attorney and asked if he would contact my sister about her plans to come for division. A day later, Chris Donovan called, "Julie denies receiving any letter." "It figures," I fumed to Brad. I decided to recheck my inventory and try to make it more complete.

The summer kitchen was where the glassware and Fostoria pieces were kept. Some appeared to be missing, about half. My inventory tweaked, I moved on to the kitchen where, for the first time, I noticed that the beautiful Victorian cup and saucer that had been designated to me was gone.

The label with my name was lying on the kitchen floor. I phoned Julie immediately. When she answered, I tried to remain calm. "We are at the house and my beautiful cup and saucer are gone."

Julie offhandedly replied, "It might have gotten broken, I just don't know. I wasn't there." I noted a discrepancy here from my information from Bob, the caretaker, who had told me that Julie was at the house frequently and no one was there without her.

"Then why is the saucer gone too?" The cup had been hanging on hooks on the kitchen wall while the saucer was kept in the cupboard.

After a long pause, Julie replied in a nasty voice, "How did *you* know where the saucer was?"

Tears stung my eyes as I hung up. What was happening? Where and when was this all going to end? Was Julie going to go on forever with her anger, resentments, and retaliations? My still, small voice told me, "Only if you let her."

After I calmed down, I continued into the dining room. The China cabinet was, once again, bare of any of Aunt Beckie's Victorian pieces and plates I had placed there. I checked the lower cabinet and Aunt Beckie's silverware was gone as well as

Mom's sterling. It had been seven months since we had moved the items from Aunt Beckie's, and at times I struggled to remember what had been in certain spots. I kicked myself mentally for not having the energy to do a thorough inventory at the time we moved these things. I had done my best, but my best had not been good enough.

I moved into my parents' old room and opened the three drawers where the antique portraits from 1850 to the early 1900s had been placed. They were empty. That meant the treasured portraits of my mother were lost to me forever. Tears stung my eyes.

I checked a fourth drawer, where the fancy pillowcases were stored. They were gone as well.

As Brad and I proceeded into the living room, the pictures from Aunt Beckie's were still hanging on the walls. From there, Brad and I ascended the stairs. The first room at the top of the stairs was the storeroom. When we opened the door to check Aunt Beckie's desk, it was wide open, drawers pulled out, writing top down, and the secret compartments within the desk wide open.

"She certainly boldly exhibits her defiance," I commented with disgust. The gold dust and brooch as well as the fancy antique death certificates of our two great grandfathers were missing, but the Victorian cards remained. I had neglected to list the gold dust, brooch and birth certificates. Later there would be repercussions about this.

The following morning, Brad suggested we go in to see Chris Donovan. When we arrived, we were ushered into his office. Chris sat in front of us, his face all business-like. He assured me everything was being done according to the book and told me I needed to take an inventory of all the things that had been removed from Aunt Beckie's place. I assured him that had already been done. He asked why these things had been moved, and I told him about my sister's phone call about a possible new state law regarding the estates of those in long-term care. "She told me to take what I wanted since it would all be gone, but I didn't do that," I said. "Nothing has ever been divided and now many things are missing from both estates. I'm trying to get division of both estates."

"This isn't about your parents' estate," the attorney replied, "but your aunt's, and you need to be accountable for what you have moved."

Brad and I left, with him saying that

Chris Donovan did not believe a word I had uttered. We went back to the attorney's office the following day and turned in the inventory. I explained my attempt to guesstimate and try to remember what had been brought over because there were items now missing from the parental home that were my aunt's. These items were enumerated to him. The attorney was polite but cool and appeared disbelieving. We left feeling misunderstood. Helpless to correct the situation, we returned to Illinois.

* * * * *

I was convinced my sister would stop at nothing to get what she wanted. Julie played by no rules except her own, and all my attempts to anticipate her behavior had always fallen short of what happened. I recalled a conversation between Mom and Aunt Beckie: "I hope Jim will keep her on the straight and narrow," my mother had said. I had one small hope that Julie would tell the truth and would bring back what she had taken. Brad was doubtful, but we decided to wait and see what would transpire at Aunt Beckie's sale.

Approximately one month later, another letter from the probate attorney arrived and he made it clear, "I do not want the two estates mixed in with your Aunt Beckie's Probate and people have been hired to ready her estate for the sale. You have listed items in the inventory that Julie states she is not aware of and, since you listed them, you must be aware of their existence." He went on to say, "Your sister wonders if you have them."

That's a laugh, I thought with disgust and read on: "They are to be returned and included in the sale."

The attorney went on to explain, "Julie found no Nippon ware at either house and claims to have only a creamer and sugar as well as a milk pitcher which is Nippon."

What a farce. Julie had a cabinet full of Nippon pieces worth a considerable amount of money that had been removed from the parental home without my consent. The creamer and sugar were Aunt Beckie's and already removed before our removal from those premises. There were several pieces of Nippon squirreled away at the parental home that had been taken from Aunt Beckie's again prior to Brad's and my moving her things to my parents' place. Did Julie intend to remove them surreptitiously later, as she had been doing for some time? The lawyer went on to explain, "Your sister has no knowledge of an antique Masonic ring you are to receive."

My grandfather's ring was not a Masonic ring. *Where did that come from?*

Was Julie trying to muddy the waters or was the attorney mixed up? I hadn't seen the ring in many years, but I knew it had been put in the safe deposit box by Mom and Dad for me and did not belong to Aunt Beckie's estate. Besides, I had told Julie where it was. She certainly wasn't volunteering to talk about our grandfather's 18K gold and diamond ring that she had in her possession. Vickie had received a letter from Julie earlier in the summer regarding the diamond she was to receive. She in turn phoned me in shock and anger that her aunt was trying to bypass me in giving out the diamonds. Another question remained. Why had Julie asked me, while staying with her, if she could have two of the three diamonds from both estates? The only answer I could come up with was that Julie would never want to admit to her girls about my generosity in agreeing to giving two diamonds to my nieces. They might just begin to question their mother.

Lastly, the attorney informed me that Julie owned the Victorian Tiffany hanging lamp, which she would remove. *It has already been removed*, I silently corrected his letter. Either the lawyer or Julie couldn't seem to get anything straight. "The Victorian mirror is yours if you want to pay for it." Finally, the attorney informed me that Julie had been allowed to buy a prize Victorian rocker ahead of time and a gorgeous floor lamp under the guise that they had to return to Williamsport forthwith. Why had Julie been allowed to do this when I had been told I could not go in to choose items from my aunt's estate until 2 p.m. on a Saturday afternoon, three weeks hence? Was I never to have any fair choice of my family's estates? I was distraught and decided to discuss the issue with Brad when he returned home that evening.

The following morning, after a thorough discussion with Brad, I wrote a letter to the attorney. I stated I had removed all items to the parental home and had nothing in my possession other than what my sister had given me. I added that I would not take anything from the estate without Julie's knowledge and consent beforehand because I knew how it felt not to be given that consideration. I requested that the things Julie had been allowed to buy ahead of time be brought back as "That didn't seem quite fair. I am contemplating doing whatever is necessary to get the personal property issue resolved and both estates settled." I ended the letter with a suggestion Brad had made, "If there can be no accord reached in the issues I have raised, I suggest we cancel the sale temporarily and get a different Representative or a court appointed arbitrator. Please confirm agreement or cancelation of date. I just want fairness!"

Several weeks later, Chris Donovan replied with a copy to Julie in which he stated my sister would return the items she had acquired early. He suggested that perhaps "each sister needs to seek independent counsel and if you are seriously concerned about incidents that have occurred, you should petition the Probate Court for supervision of your sister in order to get these matters resolved. It is unfortunate that it comes to this, because when it is all said and done, there will be legal fees, hard feelings for more than the value of the estate." He asked that each sister confirm they both wanted the sale to proceed. I called to confirm, as did Julie. The sale would be held in early August.

My concern wasn't about "hard feelings." Why would I want someone in my life who was controlling, manipulative, and dishonest? I didn't have friends who were that way or that had ever treated me as badly as my own sister. Money, because it was a small estate, was unimportant too. *Can't Donovan understand money has nothing to do with it?* I fumed. Ethics were very important to me and couldn't be weighed and balanced with money. My sister and I were worlds apart, and I was being forced to face the fact our relationship was doomed.

EIGHTEEN

THE SALE

1993

When we arrived in town for the sale, there was a waiting period of three days before we were allowed to go in. On doing so, I discovered that many of Aunt Beckie's missing items had not come back. The floor lamp and Victorian rocker had been returned, but Julie had been allowed to come to the sale at eleven that morning, prior to my two in the afternoon appointment. Why hadn't the attorney demanded Julie come back and not only choose items with me but toss a coin for items we both might want? After all that had gone on with Julie, this was like rubbing salt in my wounds. I made my choices and left, upset with the latitude the attorney had given my sister. Brad had been right. Julie was not protecting items—she had stolen joint property.

We left immediately from the sale and

went to see the probate attorney. Brad and I informed him that Julie had not returned everything she had taken from the house. He told me firmly that I needed to take my inventory list and bring back the items that were not at the sale, saying that I needed to report the whereabouts of all items and return them to the estate lady handling the sale. Also, he reprimanded me for insisting there were no antique photos at the parental home, as Faith had checked the house and there was a drawer of photos. My annoyed retort was that, if that were the case, two drawers of the antique photos were still missing.

Chris Donovan stared at me but made no reply. He couldn't help but see how exasperated and frustrated I was as I struggled to remain composed. He informed me items bought had to be paid for now, as there could be no waiting period for money until the sale of the house. He explained that was because it was different from a parental estate sale, which would not require that. That meant that when the sale ended, Julie would still get her half of all proceeds from the sale of the items and the house. I would not. We felt sure she had planned it that way.

We left the office and returned to my parents' place, where I found some items that had been overlooked when Aunt Beckie's contents were returned to her home for the sale. I brought them to the sale and crossed them off my original inventory. As I had been instructed to do by the attorney, I reported to Mary, the estate lady, what had been found and what was still missing. Mary was also the person who did the official inventory that went into the attorney's files, and she informed me they needed to be as accurate as possible. When she inquired about the items still missing, she was told these items were the best of my aunt's belongings and I explained my sister must have them, as they could not be found anywhere at our parents' home.

Someone who knew Julie had listened in on the conversation, took that conversation out of context, and reported it to a friend of Julie's who then called her. Little did my sister realize or care how effective she had been in the deceitful information she had given the attorney.

Over the course of the week-long sale, Brad and I returned to see what had been marked down each day that we might want. During one of those visits, Faith was browsing through the contents so far not sold. She approached me with a rather stern expression. "You should be fair and honest with your sister. You have no more right to these things than she does."

Why did Julie always manage to get others stirred up enough to fight for her while she sat regally in the background as the injured party? How did she do it? I answered Faith with as much sincerity and warmth in my voice as I could manage. "I don't think you understand what has really happened here, Faith, but I want you to know I would never treat my sister or anyone else dishonestly. There are probably a lot of facts you are unaware of."

Faith was staring at me intently as I finished and excused myself. Later, she approached me again and asked if Brad and I would please stop over and see her before our return to Illinois. I hesitatingly promised we would.

When the sale was over, we made an appointment with Chris Donovan. Once in his office, I updated the inventory as to the items that were still missing. He asked, "Do you have them?" When I insisted I didn't, he asked, "Are you sure of what you allege here?" I unhesitatingly told him "Yes," but his affect caused me to feel he had grave doubts about me.

I reiterated to him my mother's warning: "Once she gets things to Williamsport, you may never be able to get them back."

Unable to elicit a positive response to this situation, Brad and I left Donovan's office and returned to the car, where we sat and discussed the situation. I had to accept the fact Julie had been stealing out of the house since before our mother died. The stealing had been extended to Aunt Beckie's estate. Dad, knowing I disagreed with his and Mom's assessment of Julie, had instead told his sister Doris. No wonder all my designated items were "missing", according to Julie. *There's nothing in writing…*

I felt sure that, for Julie, there had never been a meaningful relationship, only emotional superficiality. My greatest comfort in that moment and for a long time to come was the fact my parents had tried to warn me and avoid a disaster. I was deeply touched that they had looked into my soul and knew who I really was. They must have known I could not do what my sister was doing to me. I made a silent vow to pursue the division of all property and get out from under the expense of my parents' home somehow.

Brad had been right again. Chris Donovan did not appear to believe me and now it was a question of how to force division of my parents' estate. I asked what could be done, unable to believe there was any real effective avenue to pursue. Brad said, "Get your own attorney." Chris Donovan had also suggested this. I asked if we shouldn't try to talk to Jim first, but Brad assured me he would be impervious to my position. We made an appointment with Cyrus Peters for the following afternoon.

* * * * *

We were greeted by a tall, slender, gray-haired and pleasant man who listened intently to my story. He had been a former prosecuting attorney, and I noted that he was very quick to pick up details and remember them as the discussion grew in complexity and length. He was told about the parental estate, designated items never dispersed but missing, my mother's sterling gone. Now, all my aunt's silver was gone and an old silver-plate set of my mother's had been returned to my parents' house. Cyrus smiled knowingly. "Aunt Beckie's silverware must have been nicer than your mother's silver-plate."

Cyrus asked, "Have you ever been informed by your sister that division needed to take place within two years after the death of your father?" My answer was no but volunteered that I had agreed to postpone division because my sister was so evasive and vague when I asked. I strongly felt something was terribly wrong but didn't feel alert enough to deal with it. When he had taken down the information, he declined a retainer, stating he wanted to speak with the probate attorney first before deciding whether to take the case. My heart sank.

When we left, Brad assured me he would take it and he did. Cyrus was stern during this next visit, and imparted instructions to me, "You will have to listen to what you are told. I don't want to tell you something a dozen times for you to get it! And I want you to get things right, not mixed up."

Stunned, I kept silent. Julie had worked her magic with the probate attorney. Cyrus told me he would need my father's will and papers. I agreed to send them upon our return to Illinois. Cyrus asked, "Why did Julie decide to take your father's probate out of the county, which in the end, has prevented inherent oversight? That is illegal. Your father's legal residence was here, was it not?"

"She asked me if I had any objections," I replied, "and I asked if she could legally do that, and she assured me she could. She said it would save her making trips to the hometown." Suddenly I connected the dots and remembered that Julie and Jim came home once a month to visit Aunt Beckie, even after Dad had passed away. I related this fact to Cyrus.

"She wouldn't have had to come here that often to take care of probate business," he said. "Once a month would have been adequate. Moving the probate out of the county shouldn't have been done, and I suspect she knew that." Then another smile crossed his pleasant face and he added, "Representatives should be as pure as the driven snow, and probate procedure should be followed." He assured me Chris Donovan was a very honest man but seemed puzzled as to why he had declined to handle the situation in Aunt Beckie's estate. Brad and I had felt that Donovan hated controversy. Cyrus ended the session with his promise to look into the matter thoroughly and advise us. Brad assured him that we would be available anytime he needed us to be there but requested a few days' notice.

After we left the office, I asked Brad to be at every session so there would be no misunderstandings in what I was being told. He looked disgusted. "Julie is doing her best to make you seem impossible to deal with. You just aren't that bad. What better way to discredit you than by claiming you are mentally inept and misunderstand everything?"

In spite of this negative element, I felt relief that someone would deal with Julie on my behalf. I was at a dead end in trying to cope with my sister. Would she seem as impossible to Cyrus Peters as she had seemed to me? Time would tell.

* * * * *

As promised, Brad and I went to Faith's home before leaving for Illinois. Faith met us at the door and was very warm and welcoming. She opened up as soon as we were seated: "I have been thinking about your comments to me at the sale, and I remember that each time your sister entered your Aunt Beckie's house when I was there, I saw her carry out something. One time, it was the blue brocade tablecloth. Another time it was Victorian bowls, and she seemed to be switching things in the curio cabinet."

"When you helped my sister pack the items that were to be moved back to Aunt Beckie's for the sale, were the Victorian plates, the antique Victorian pictures, and the sliver gone?"

"I don't remember seeing the silver," Faith replied, "but the plates were packed to go back. The pictures I didn't see."

"Well, those items never made it to the sale."

"There were times when I would check the house after your sister was there and find things gone." Then she added, "I must tell you, she came over here all upset about the mirror when you moved it. She wanted to know the condition of the mirror prior to its removal. I told her that it had been moved intact, and the missing pieces had been gone for a very long time. It had been that way for years and wasn't from moving."

I thanked Faith for the information, then I asked if she had spoken to Julie by phone the week that all Aunt Beckie's things were moved. Faith looked puzzled. "No, I never spoke to Julie until she came to town the other day. Why?"

I told her about Julie's accusation that I had made off with a "chest full of silver." Faith assured me that she had never told Julie any such thing.

"Did Jason have to crawl through the basement window with high boots on due to high water in the basement because Brad shut off a light that the sump pump was connected to?"

Faith laughed. "No. Did Julie tell you that?"

"Yes."

"There was only one inch of water, and he just stepped inside the door and flipped on the switch. You have to turn out the lightbulb by hand." Then she added, "What an exaggeration!"

"I am at the end of my patience with her," I said. "We tried to do an inventory and set a good example as to how joint property should be handled, and we tried to set a date for division of all things at our parents'. All our efforts were ignored, and all she could do was take more valuable and cherished items and accuse me of stealing. I just want things divided, so we have consulted an attorney."

"Who?"

"Cyrus Peters."

"He's good. Will you go to court?"

"We don't know. If she cooperates, we won't have to."

"Please come and see me and let me know how things are progressing."

Brad and I said our goodbyes and left.

*　　*　　*　　*　　*

We collected all of the records that Cyrus requested. I enclosed a letter apprising him of extra details not related in our first meeting, such as my sister's penchant of a double standard, one for herself, and a different one for me, the details about the car, and other matters. I also informed him of the confidential letter I had written to Chris Donovan.

A week after our return to Illinois, Julie called. "I'm going to take Mother's Noritake dishes for Elizabeth and the buggy."

"You are not going to remove anything else from the house," I commanded in an even but very firm tone. "You leave everything right there."

"Are you telling me I can't take *my* buggy?"

"It's part of the estate and should be itemized."

"I can't take *my* buggy!" Julie repeated, her voice elevated.

"It should be itemized, but I will think about it."

Julie hung up. The buggy wasn't an issue for me. I wrote Julie a letter:

"You, being the first born, played with the buggy first, but you weren't an only child, Julie. All the years I played with it, Mother called it my buggy. In later years, she called it "the buggy you girls played with." Sometimes, she still called it "your buggy" when speaking to me. She may have done the same in your presence. All the grandchildren played with it, including Vickie. When she was three, Mother offered to let her take it home and for a while she had it at our place. I have always thought of it as "ours". However, no buggy is worth a disagreement. The last thing I want to do is fight over a buggy, so you may remove it from the house, as well as Mother's twelve Noritake place settings for Liz."

NINETEEN

CONFRONTATION

1993

Three weeks after the sale in August, we returned as Brad's brother Bill had passed. On this trip, we were allowed to use my parents' place. We planned to stay for the week. I became more concerned I would never get anything of my mother's at the rate things were disappearing from the house. I phoned Cy at his office.

"Can items I would like to be inventoried and stored at your office?"

"No," he replied, "you can't do that, but I will tell you what you can legally do. Make an inventory of the things you want and give the list to your sister. Keep a copy for yourself."

I hung up, relieved that there was some avenue to pursue, but still felt a nagging fear Julie would take any items listed and claim that the items didn't exist, or that she was protecting them. I chose a few items, found boxes in closets and emptied them, rummaged through the laundry room and found newspapers in which to wrap things. I packed up my designated Roseville teapot with its creamer and sugar bowl, as well as my mother's old damask cloth. Julie still had the one she had stolen from my home. In finishing the packing, some glass bowls were added but I noted some were missing. Grandmother's Victorian plates, of course, were gone. An alabaster lighthouse as well as the two most ornate oil lamps had also disappeared. Listed on my inventory were several pieces of Mom's pottery she had acquired in Mexico, but I didn't pack them. The boxes were placed in the second downstairs bedroom, the one in which I hadn't been allowed to sleep.

Both my sister and I had been designated certain pieces of furniture, but Julie didn't want her portion. My pieces had been placed on the probate which indicated to me she knew they were to be given.

With the packing finished, I copied my list and wrote my sister a letter. I said that I had requested, on a number of occasions, to equally divide family items where each of us could make choices together. I reminded her that she had declined each time. "Therefore, I have prepared a detailed list of what is left of our parents' items that

I wish to have, as I have nothing from the house. Anything removed from our home should always be agreed upon by both of us. Please check through the list, and the boxes if you wish, and check off the items that you agree I can remove."

Later that afternoon, Cyrus' office called. He wanted to see me on our way out of the state on Friday. The phone at my parents' home had rung periodically during our stay, and when we would answer, no one was there. Brad deduced that Julie and Jim were, once again, anxiously awaiting out departure so they could check the house and make sure nothing had been stolen. Was my sister aware that I had contacted an attorney? I left the list of items with a note on the kitchen table

* * * * *

We arrived promptly for our morning appointment with Cyrus. He had a lot of news. "Julie has admitted to Chris she has not had division nor informed you it was to be done within the two-year period," he said. "She never explained how probate was to proceed."

He repeated that Julie had no right to take probate out of the county, as Dad had lived here all his life and all his property and money were here. "Probate business could not have required any more visits than their usual time here," he added. "Now, I have explained to you about your aunt's house," Cyrus began to speak but I interrupted him.

"No, I don't know anything about the house."

His voice became sharp; "I told you that you were going to have to listen to what I tell you and keep things straight!"

Brad interrupted, "Cy, we haven't heard anything about the house, and I have been here every time she has."

Cyrus's tone became apologetic. "Oh, well, then this is the whole story. The house has been on the market for just under three months. Julie got an offer that was one-third of the asking price, made no counteroffers, and without informing you, accepted the offer and went even further. She accepted a check as a down payment. What do you think?"

"If she's going to give it away, give it to me," Brad said. "She did the same thing with the lakefront property. You would think Josie didn't need money. Julie has done everything she can to make it difficult for her financially, and she can never work again. She was furious when Josie started getting disability payments and began to be able to pay the expenses at the parental home."

"A game player, eh?" Cy laughed softly.

"So it seems," Brad agreed. "But I have to admit, she makes a good initial impression."

Cy continued, "We can stop the sale if you disagree with her actions, but you will have to go to court and bid against the people who gave the down payment." We agreed the sale should be stopped. "I have to admit this house business is crazy," he added. "It is as if she is trying to give it away. We'll just stop the sale. I will let you know when we are to go to court."

We departed the office and set out for Vickie's. Vickie and I had a doctor's appointment, and I would stay with her until Brad came to visit, which was usually about every three weeks.

*   *   *   *   *

Ever since I had become aware of Julie's motives and actions, Vickie had been a different person, probably feeling vindicated for what she sensed in her aunt. One Saturday afternoon, the phone rang: it was Aunt Doris. She wasn't sure where I was and had accidentally reached me at Vickie's. She sounded irritable and coolly asked how I was. I assured her I was feeling better and was to see the doctor that week.

"Well," she said, "you've *really* done it now! You have nobody, and your sister took such good care of you!"

I replied that yes, my sister had taken good care of me, but that I had paid her. Aunt Doris was silent for a moment before replying, "Well, I didn't know that."

I hoped some of the hot air had gone out of her sails, but after a few moments, Aunt Doris regained her momentum and carried on, somehow determined to vindicate Julie. She related a story about her hairdresser, who took care of her mother and her mother lived with her. When her mother died, the will left only two-thirds to her and one-third to the other daughter. She said irritably, "She should be given all of it!"

I didn't know the whole story, but replied, "Inheritance is a gift, not a right, Aunt Doris. The problem arises when the heirs don't follow the will and proper probate procedures."

Undeterred, Aunt Doris went on to another story about someone else whose mother gave everything she had to a disabled child and no other child got anything. "What a terrible thing," she wailed, "even if the others are well off, and they are, that shouldn't make any difference." I did not reply but wondered if Aunt Doris felt that Julie had somehow been mistreated. She went on: "There are no Christmas dishes, you know."

This issue wasn't one I cared to get involved in, but after I refused Mom's offer of the Christmas dishes, she said she would give them to Alison, and I had passed that information on to my niece. Later, Julie had given the set to Liz, and it would appear she was trying to cover it up. How did Aunt Doris get involved? "You were never there at Christmas time, but Mother kept them in the cupboard beside the dishwasher." There was a long silence, then Aunt Doris said an abrupt goodbye and hung up.

The following week, Vickie and I went to our appointments with the doctor. First, we had our bloodwork done. The tests were almost normal, with only a few enlarged red blood cells. The white cells were now normal in number. However, the hematologist informed us that Vickie had a much more severe illness than I did.

When we were finished, we went upstairs to my friend Sharon's office. The company she worked for was in the same building. It was later in the afternoon, and we thought if we waited, we could catch dinner with her, but she had taken the day off. We had a fun dinner out anyway and returned home on the train.

Sharon got the message that we had visited and called me the next morning. She asked how I was doing, and I told her my bloodwork looked good.

"You were back home in Michigan, weren't you?"

When I responded positively, Sharon continued, "What is happening there?"

I spoke about Aunt Beckie, whom Sharon had as a teacher, and then I volunteered that moving things out of my aunt's place to the parental home had turned into a fiasco.

"What a sad thing," she replied. "It must have been a lot of work—at least the state won't get it. Julie should have been pleased."

"The problem is that Julie is accusing me of stealing from the things we moved, and I didn't. I never dreamed she would react this way."

"I have heard that there are problems between you two. Eunice," Sharon said, referring to her sister, "has always been close to Doris, and they talk often on the phone. What is the problem?"

I explained about Julie's refusal to give me my designated items and the rest of it. Upon hearing the details, Sharon said, "Anyone who could do that to their own sister is evil! You ought to get the probate court involved. That's how I got my inheritance, or I would have been cheated out of money. There were no cherished or valuable items."

"We already are doing that."

"Good!" Sharon responded with enthusiasm. Then she confided, "Be very careful what you tell Doris, because she is saying terrible things about you. Josie, I mean really terrible things."

"Like what?"

"You don't want to know. They are really awful."

"I don't talk to Aunt Doris about anything."

"Well, I am just telling you, be extremely careful. She seems to have no conscience about badmouthing you. Don't talk to her or else blast her. She deserves it!"

"I send her birthday cards, and call her from time to time, but I couldn't blast her. She is eighty years old, and I am not going to get into it with her."

"She is not too old to be a nasty, vicious old lady," Sharon argued.

Sharon made me promise to keep her informed of developments and let her know how I was feeling. After we hung up, I reflected on our conversation. It seemed Sharon knew who I really was better than my own sister. On the issue of Aunt Doris, I felt I must continue to send her cards and communicate on a purely social level. In spite of Julie being her favorite niece, Aunt Doris had always been kind to me, and "more is wrought by kindness."

*   *   *   *   *

Brad arrived for his weekend visit at Vickie's, after which we went home. Three weeks later, a letter arrived from Cy with a copy of a letter he had received from the probate attorney. The hearing before the judge for the house sale was scheduled for December 22. The attorney went on to say that I had packed some six boxes which "she apparently asserts are her property."

I felt totally frustrated at this take on my request. Julie knew very well what those boxes represented. Fortunately, Cy had been informed of the boxes and itemized list, as well as the letter explaining my intent, not claiming ownership. The letter continued with the fact that there were things in the house that were Julie's gifts to Mother. Either the attorney had it mixed up or Julie, as usual, was having a hard time telling the truth.

The letter ended with discussion about inheritance taxes and filing dates, as well as the report of the sale of Aunt Beckie's house verifying that Julie had accepted the low offer and had taken a down payment without consulting anyone. Once again, I was struck by her recurring behavior. Get the most out of me she could but give away or steal the contents and property that might financially benefit me. Unfortunately, there was no avenue to pursue in dad's estate thanks to no oversight by the court.

Several days later, I wrote Julie a letter: *I don't want to compound the hurt and injustices that have already occurred. My slow awakening as my condition improved to what the sister I adored was really about has been one of the most painful realizations of my life. What has happened is a sad commentary on what Mom and Dad stood for and taught us and your actions are a confirmation of their worst fears about you. You are very aware I was not declaring the items I asked for as mine. How disingenuous of you. However, you may remove the gifts you state you gave mother, but I would remind you that either your memory is faulty, or you willfully distorted the truth. Those gifts were paid for by and given by dad to mom.*

Several days later, a letter arrived from Alison. She stated she had told her mother of our many phone conversations and said she was trying to look at the recent events objectively but was sure her mother had never been dishonest with me. My hope was that she would stand by her mother, yet continue to assess her accurately, but silently, and accept the fact she simply was not the person she presented herself to be. Sadly, it appeared she had been sucked in by Julie's charming deceit.

In my reply, I wrote that I appreciated her input. My letter ended with "*Someday I hope you will want to apprise yourself of all the facts. Only then will you come to a better understanding about what has really happened.*" I signed the letter "With love." Alison was my godchild and I hoped for all good things for her.

*   *   *   *   *

A short time later, in September, Cy called to say that my sister wouldn't give an inch and refused to discuss anything. "She is a major problem. When things don't go her way, she refuses to cooperate and walks out rather than negotiate." Then he asked me to be at a meeting between my sister and myself, with both attorneys present. He voiced the hope something could be worked out between us at that time. He was assured I would be able to meet my sister on the specified date in October.

Five weeks later, we were again on our

way to Michigan for my meeting with Julie. We informed Cy that we preferred to stay at my parents' house. She agreed as she and Jim planned to drive over the day of the meeting and return home the same day.

The morning after our arrival, as I wandered through the house checking and hoping Julie would return the things she had taken, I found some of Aunt Beckie's silverware had been returned! Immediately, I called Cy to inform him a set of silverware had been returned but nothing else.

"That's because Chris told her she had to return the silver or else there could possibly be criminal charges filed against her," he explained.

I was shocked. Apparently both attorneys were going to try to make this situation right, but I had no intention of taking any actions in that regard. On the other hand, I would do whatever the process of probate required. Cy went on to explain that, if the silver had not come back, they would have had to assume I took it. They had started with Julie. Two of the four boxes of Mom's sterling had been returned.

Without consent from Julie, I could not legally remove that item, even though Julie had removed the other two boxes. Julie was in violation of probate law and lied to the attorney, stating Mom had only two boxes of sterling silver. I insisted there were four, but Chris chose to believe Julie.

Faith arrived that afternoon and together we sorted through Aunt Beckie's silver. Cy had told me to inventory the silverware item by item, and with Faith's help, that got done. She informed me that the knives, forks, and spoons from my aunt's best silverware set were still missing. Strangely enough, Julie had returned the salad forks and serving pieces. She must have been afraid to take the whole set. She had also taken six dessert forks from another set of Aunt Beckie's. The other silverware set was intact except for one soup spoon. Faith assured me there had always been six soup spoons, not five. *Games, games, games...*

The following day, Brad remained in the waiting area outside Cy's office while the meeting was held. Chris Donovan arrived with Julie and we began. Chris started things off by stating that Julie wished to have two diamonds, and I would get one. I nodded in agreement. Nothing was said about diamonds going to the girls. Julie offered me our mother's diamond ring; the other stones, which were Aunt Beckie's, were loose. I declined and chose one of Aunt Beckie's, the slightly larger one in karats and better clarity. I asked Chris how I could be sure this was the correct stone. Chris declined to answer, but Julie said, "They are correctly marked. I just want you to trust me."

I slowly rose from my chair and stood directly in front of her, looking down at her intently. "How can I trust you when you take my things?" I asked softly with a tinge of sadness.

Julie lowered her head, her eyes cast downward toward the floor. Perhaps she was experiencing some pangs of healthy shame and regret for her actions. I wished she would open up, apologize and offer to have a fair division. That was the kind of sister I had always believed I had.

Unfortunately, that kind of humility was not in Julie. The moment passed, and I returned to my chair, picked up the bag of silverware and the inventory, carried them to the attorney's desk and placed them there. "Some silverware has been returned, but some is still missing, part of my aunt's best set. Here is the inventory." I handed the list to Cy.

"There are probably pieces missing because you took them!" Julie snapped. Stealing is one thing but falsely accusing someone else is quite another.

"Now, we know that isn't true, don't we Julie?" I felt strangely calm, clearheaded, and strong. At last, I was ready to take her on.

"What about what *you* have taken?" Julie countered defiantly. She may have been able to fool her family with that kind of talk, but I felt sure the lawyers weren't buying it.

"I have not taken anything. You took the silverware, Julie."

"No, I didn't! Maybe Mary, the estate lady, stole them as well as the matching candleholders." She looked at Chris and he said, "No, the matching candleholders were sold at the sale."

"Well, Mary probably took the silverware."

How ludicrous! Julie had returned some of the silver and blamed the still missing pieces on the estate lady, who had a spotless reputation. "No, she is a very honest person. She wouldn't do that." Once again, Julie looked at Chris and he nodded in agreement with me.

"Well, I don't have it and you can't prove anything!"

Chris' and Cy's expressions were interesting: Chris looked shocked. Whatever his belief in my sister, he clearly wasn't expecting this. Cy looked amused as though he knew all the time what my sister was made of. Julie looked triumphant, seemingly totally unaware, as was I, of what a telling statement she had just made. I looked at her. "I'm not trying to prove anything, Julie. I just want fair division."

"What have *you* taken?!" she asked once more, trying to seize control of a situation that had gotten out of hand.

"I haven't taken anything. If you don't trust me, then do you think Brad would let me take anything? He is honest and fair, and you know it! Now, I would like to discuss the car issue, because you said the lawyer told you the car had to appear on the probate and therefore, I would have to pay for the car, in spite of the fact it was supposed to be a gift. It didn't have to appear on the probate. You lied to me."

"I don't know what you are talking about!"

"Yes, you do, and I have the letter right here." I pulled the letter from my briefcase. Julie's face remained blank. I rose from my chair, placed the letter on Cy's desk, and stood there.

Cy leafed briefly through the letter and looked at Julie: "Cars do not have to appear on the probate and no attorney would ever tell you that," he firmly informed her. Julie remained silent.

"You never inform me of anything, you don't tell me the truth, you take without asking. You have said that everything is yours and your father's and you don't have to tell me anything." I sounded intense.

Julie was adamant. "I didn't say that or do any of that!"

I walked over to her again. "You certainly did! Don't lie, Julie. It doesn't become you. And Jim says I ask a lot of questions? I have every right to ask as many questions as I want! Who do you people think you are?"

Julie attempted to mount an offensive: "You have been spreading rumors around town that I have stolen things from the estates. You had better be careful what you say, or I will take you to court and sue you because you can't prove a thing!" There it was again, the same words, the same sneer, only delivered more aggressively.

I didn't know what she was talking about, but I sensed I could not let Julie's offensive stand. I shot back, "Well, Julie, I call a thief, a thief! Dad knew you were stealing from the house."

"That's not true!" she spat.

"Well, he certainly did! He told Brad!"

"*No...he...didn't!*"

"Go ask Brad. He's sitting right out there in the waiting room. He will tell you exactly what Dad said to him!"

"He must have misunderstood." Trying to regain momentum, Julie added, "You moved all that stuff from Aunt Beckie's and stole a lot of it."

"Julie, you called us and told us it would all be gone by the end of the year. We thought we were being helpful."

"I didn't call you," she lied.

Once again, I pointed to the outer door: "You called me, and you called Brad at his office. Do you want me to call him in here so he can tell you what you told him?" Julie hung her head and didn't reply. I returned to my chair and removed a small box from my briefcase that contained the junk and costume jewelry Julie had given me in the name of "All there is." Feeling calmer, I took a deep breath and continued: "I would like to talk about the designated jewelry."

Before I could finish, Julie quickly rose from her chair. "I don't have to listen to any more of this!" She stormed out of the room.

"No, I didn't think you would want to talk about the jewelry!" I called out, my words following her out the door.

Julie stopped and looked at Brad, who had been reading as he waited. "Did Dad ever tell you I was taking things from the house?"

Brad looked at her with a direct,

somber gaze. "Yes, he did."

Again, she repeated the same theme, "Well, Dad must have misunderstood." She then walked out of the office.

Chris Donovan rose to his feet and walked over to me with a look I had never seen before. He looked sad, perhaps for my sister's and my broken relationship, but I also had the distinct feeling he believed me now.

"I'm sorry," I apologized, "but there is so much unsettled business from the last probate and if you could see the things she has taken from our home..."

"I guess we will see you in court," Chris replied solemnly and left the room.

TWENTY

PREPARATION AND COURT

1993

Later, when we were alone, Brad asked what had transpired during the meeting. When I related the events, Brad was shocked at Julie's brashness. "She said you can't prove a thing. Are you sure?" When I assured him that Julie had said just that, not once, but twice, Brad replied, "She'd better not say that in front of a judge, or her ass is grass!" When I expressed my concerns about the possibility of ruining any chance of a fair division because of my confrontations, Brad assured me there was never any hope of that anyway. "She is the way she is."

Puzzled at the accusations Julie had thrown my way, I told Brad I wanted to stop and see Faith. Maybe she could explain what was going on.

We stopped at Faith's the following day. She seemed happy to see us and invited us in. She questioned Brad and me about the meeting, so we related some details. I asked about Julie's accusation regarding my spreading rumors that she had stolen things from the estates. I continued laughingly, "I didn't have a clue what she was talking about, but I told her I call a thief, a thief!"

Brad interjected, "You can't sue someone for telling the truth."

"What happened is that Naomi Johnstone listened in on your conversation with Mary and heard you say your sister must have taken the Victorian plates. She, in turn, told Greta Endicott, who called your sister," Faith volunteered.

"I was ordered by the probate attorney to report to Mary anything I couldn't find that was on my inventory I had done when we moved all Aunt Beckie's belongings. As awful as Julie has been, I would never say a word to anyone here." We conversed a while longer. When we left, Faith urged us to stay in touch.

*　　*　　*　　*　　*

Several days later, Cy called and asked us to come to his office. When we arrived, he informed me that Chris Donovan was suggesting an Inquiry.

"What is that?" I asked.

"A Judicial Inquiry is an investigation that will give the Judge added information when he sits before you and your sister. Court is the next step since your sister walked out of the meeting and has been uncooperative. The judge has a right to hold inquires before he rules."

I assured Cy I had no objection to an Inquiry. He asked if I had any objection to them speaking to anyone in town who knew or was close to Aunt Beckie and my parents. I assured him I didn't. All issues settled, we departed Cy's office and the next day left for Illinois.

Once we were home, I busied myself with preparing the probate attorney's requested list of items that had been at Aunt Beckie's home but weren't at the sale. As I wrote the letter and listed the items, I explained that some of the items were at the parental home at the time of my aunt's funeral but were missing when Brad and I returned the following spring. I listed twenty items but could have listed more. I knew that what I had listed, along with issues related earlier in my private letter to Chris, would be looked at during the Inquiry and later in court, probably in the judge's chambers. Julie would have to prepare a similar list and discuss her issues. I couldn't imagine what my sister would put on her list as I hadn't stolen anything. My sister had already tried to paint a picture of me as inept, slow, and dishonest, judging from Chris Donovan's first reactions to me. I sealed the letter with the hope that those who take things surreptitiously should have to pay the fair market value instead of the estate value.

* * * * *

Several weeks after our return, we planned to leave again for Michigan: after all, it was hunting season. Once again, Brad packed the car without the usual back seat bed, as I wanted to try sitting up all the way and perhaps take a nap in a semi-sitting position during the long ride. Feeling better, I was less fearful of physical stress of the trip. Vickie accompanied us. We phoned Julie to inform her we wanted to use the house and she consented. Cy had phoned as well, asking when we would be returning. We arranged an appointment at his office for the following day.

We arrived promptly at the attorney's office, and Cy ushered us in. He took a seat behind his desk and gestured for us to be seated. Vickie had accompanied us this time as she had not met Cy. He began, "The Inquiry has been completed. I think you should know that absolutely everything you claimed has been corroborated and verified except the plates that were at your aunt's. Faith claims only eighteen."

I corrected him, "Faith has forgotten about the other plates in the house. There were eighteen plates of my grandmother's in my aunt's buffet. There were five more hanging on the walls and two to three on each shelf, one in the living room and one in the dining room were from her husband's family. Faith apparently forgot to count them. Besides that, there was a bowl that I also was counting. What was left for the sale was the least of the plates and were actually my aunt's mother-in-law's and not as beautiful. Obviously, they don't hold the same sentimentality for me."

"It's too bad you didn't do an inventory. It is a valuable tool in assessing what is missing."

"I did, but it wasn't detailed enough. I didn't list each plate and its maker, nor did I list each piece of silverware. Anyway, I feel sure my sister would have found a way to get around it."

Cy shook his head in the affirmative and then leaned forward over his desk. "Your sister said and did everything she could to try to make you look bad. When we looked into it, nothing she alleged turned out to be true. She is your sister and will always be your sister, but she isn't a very nice person. I am convinced she will continue to say and do almost anything to make you look bad and I think you should be aware of this."

I was thankful for the warning but felt helpless to change things. My best tool was to continue to be as honest and open as possible.

Cy continued, half smiling now as he peered over his half glasses. "Chris was saying that you are both just lovely girls. I said, Now wait Chris, how can someone who has acted as Julie has be a lovely person? You are saying black is white but black isn't white. Black is black and white is white and your client is not a lovely person. I suspect she has won him over with her charm."

"But your sister won't budge and absolutely has no sense of fairness. I've never seen anything like it. She has absolutely no idea what fairness is. I tried to meet with her and Chris. She was a problem. She wouldn't look at me nor speak to me and refused to be in the same room. Usually, family members each give a little until a compromise is reached. In all my years working with families, I have never had anyone stonewall like your sister."

Vickie spoke for the first time, "That's

because she knows you have her number." Everyone chuckled.

"I always underestimate her," I said.

"She's a gameplayer and I don't know if Chris gets it," Cy added.

"Will he tell her how badly she came out in the Inquiry?" I asked.

"I hope so, but I don't know. Sometimes I wonder if he doesn't like confronting her." He gave me Julie's list with all her allegations toward me. I was to look through them and be prepared to answer questions about the list in court. Court would convene in early December. I stiffened inside and hoped against hope I would be able to function with alertness. Cy told Brad he could be present for the proceedings and then began to devise a strategy. He informed me that what transpired in court was the window-dressing that had some influence on the judge's decision, but that the results of the Inquiry and the arguments by the attorneys in chambers would have the most influence.

I felt buoyed by this bit of information and began to worry less about my sluggish mental faculties.

"I also think we should challenge her honesty as a Representative," Cy went on. "Either we should put her out or put her on supervision. The problem with putting her out is that there is no one else to do the Representative's work. You are too ill and live too far away. We will deal with that in court. Now, the matter of the sale of your aunt's house. You plan to be here to bid against the people who have placed a down payment on it, is that correct?" We nodded.

Brad volunteered, "She did the same thing with the lakeshore property. She gave it away."

Cy looked disgusted at this, then continued: "The question is, how to get to your sister. I am very angry about this house situation. They monopolize it, and when they called and even insisted on using it in the winter too, I just blew up at Chris."

"They always monopolize the house. Time of year doesn't seem to matter. They could have stayed at Jim's mother's house when their family isn't here and let us stay at the parental home, but it's not grand enough for my sister."

"I didn't know there was another house they could use. I think she must be obsessed with your parents' place."

"She certainly is," Brad agreed.

Cy grinned. "Maybe we should try to break the obsession."

"Do whatever you think should be

done," I said.

"Okay, we will go for breaking the obsession. I've wondered about that, but I knew you girls have all your childhood belongings in that house and I just didn't know if you were up to doing that."

"It's alright," I said. "Maybe they will have an idea how it feels to pay and not be allowed to use it."

"She removed a hanging Tiffany lamp from Rebecca's house," Brad said, "and in light of all she has removed from the house I would suggest that she have it appraised. The appraisal she did do is a lie. It is a 36-inch hanging lamp, not a 22-inch, and Josie's grandfather bought it at an estate sale at a mansion in Cleveland, Ohio years ago. It's likely a Tiffany, as Abigail always called it that, but it could be a Handel or a Pierpont, any of those of that quality."

"I would like to ask the judge for a ruling so they would have to pay fair market value instead of probate value." I was silent as I wasn't in agreement with either of them. The lamps were designated items, but for the moment I let it slide. Cy seemed to like the idea and added it to his notes. If the judge ruled in my favor on that request, Julie would be able to see that I could have done that but didn't. The last thing I wanted was to appear vengeful.

We returned to my parents' home and reviewed the list Cy had given me. I was at a loss as to what Julie was talking about in some of the thirteen items she had listed. In one instance, it seemed she was trying to challenge my possession of my maternal grandmother's bracelet that Mom had given me when I was fourteen. The only thing I could think to do was to call Faith. I wasn't sure she could be of any help but felt sure she would know the answers to some of these questionable items.

I got Faith on the phone. First on the list were five spritzer bottles that had supposedly disappeared from one of the bedrooms. I had purchased one at a sale, but I hadn't seen any others. Faith stated there had been only three, but my aunt had given away two of them sometime before and Faith gave me the names of those individuals. Roseville pottery was the next item that Julie had described as very valuable. After hearing Faith's description, I knew I had seen only three pieces and they had been cracked. Julie was claiming there were four and all were missing. Faith went on to verify that all had been cracked, all three pieces, not four, and that Rebecca had given her a small piece one year as a Christmas present. The pieces were an ugly brown and about the most unattractive pottery I had ever seen. Laughingly, Faith agreed. I would not have wanted any even if given to me.

Another item on Julie's list was her maternal grandparents' dinnerware, blue and white Stoke England colonial pottery. I could remember the dinnerware and had eaten from that set many times during my childhood but had not seen any at the house. Faith assured me there weren't any pieces that had survived down through the years. Julie claimed there were only a few pieces moved to the parental home and claimed they were still there, but I never saw them.

Julie's next item was fabric of our grandmother's that had come from her heavy, brocade curtains. I was totally disgusted at Julie's attempt to call this stolen. She had removed the large tablecloth made from that beautiful fabric from Aunt Beckie's home following her admission to the long-term care facility. On finding the old paper bag in the back bedroom, along with the ten down pillows and a quilt that needed repair, my friend Laurie had offered to wash and recover the pillows, repair the quilt, and cut from the shredded curtain material a small, four-by-five piece of fabric and make me a tablecloth. I had thought nothing about it because Julie had taken the finer one. The quilt had been sold at the sale and the pillows sold later.

Julie claimed that silverware was missing but said only forty pieces were gone and noted that no silverware had been present at the estate sale. *I wonder why...* Faith was asked about my grandfather's pocket watch, noting that years ago my father had been given our maternal grandfather's watch. Now Julie was alleging I had it? I knew nothing about a pocket watch. Faith explained that no one had access to jewelry as it had all been kept in a safe deposit box. Only the Representative had access.

The next item was a painting by Jim Lee: "Vase of Flowers." I knew of such a picture that had hung in Aunt Beckie's living room and had asked Julie where it was. She denied there had ever been a picture hanging there. Faith partially agreed with Julie and said there hadn't been a picture there for a long time. Aunt Beckie used to tell us a story that had always been very interesting to me. There were two Jim Lee oil paintings when Aunt Beckie taught art in a Detroit high school early in her teaching career. She had Jim Lee as an art student, and she thought he was exceptionally talented. Growing up, we had heard wonderful stories about how his immigrant parents had twelve children and owned a laundry. Each child had to pledge that, after finishing college, he would help the next child through. As a result, all their children had college educations. A picture of the family and their story had appeared in a major newspaper and Aunt Beckie had saved the clipping. She told us Jim Lee eventually had showings in New York City. Aunt Beckie had given one of the two paintings to Mom but had kept the second rendering, which I liked better. Some years ago, there had been an antique dealer who came to her door because he heard she had many fine pieces. She sold some things to him. Had that been one of them?

On accessing the internet, there was an artist named Jim Lee, but he was too young to be the Jim Lee my aunt had known. *Where was the painting now?*

Julie's next items were the missing oil lamps. The most beautiful ones were missing from both estates. I had no oil lamps, but they had never been one of my priorities. Julie was informed where Aunt Beckie's three were during her tirades. The best one was gone, and now she's trying to blame me for that? How despicable!

Now it was Faith's turn to ask a

question. "Why didn't the pillows show up at the sale?" I explained Julie had been informed there were ten down pillows that needed to be washed and re-covered and that my friend Laurie, whom Faith had met, had done it for nothing. Laurie lived near Brad's brother and, when she was finished, she packed them in several boxes, gave them to Bill, who brought them to the farm. Brad had taken them to my parents' house at my request. He had put the boxes in the back bedroom closet and never mentioned them again. In the flurry preceding Aunt Beckie's sale, the boxes had been completely overlooked. I went on to explain that I inadvertently stumbled across those boxes in the back closet. Only then did I remember how they had gotten there, and I did not know what to do with them. Aunt Beckie's sale was over, so I left five for Julie and removed five to Brad's. Later, I testified to this in court.

With all the questions answered, I thanked Faith. She, in turn, asked that I call or come over after court.

*   *   *   *   *

We returned to Illinois. We only had about three weeks before we had to return for the hearing. A few days later, Brad called Julie to check if we could use the house. Everything was shut down at the farm as it was early December and cold weather had moved in. We hoped they would drive over for the day or stay at Jim's mother's house since there were only two of them, but Julie informed him they would be using the house. Brad made reservations for a motel room.

Morning came too soon. I struggled to be alert, tired from the long trip the day before. I drank my protein drink and had some coffee, readied myself, unable to stand any food on my nervous stomach. In spite of everything, I felt blessed knowing Brad would support me throughout the hearing. Julie would be legally confronted about her behavior. Sometimes I was barely able to bring myself to read the correspondence from the attorney and I would make Brad read it to me. The stress had been terrific and now this was the only avenue left. I had prayed about it and even dreamed one night that my mother appeared to me. I had asked her what should be done, troubled that I had to go this far to get a settlement from Julie. Mom had answered me in the dream to keep doing what I was doing. That dream had made a deep impression on me. There was this strong feeling I had actually spoken to my mother, whose presence I had felt several times before, with a strong aroma of fresh cut flowers, once when I was in such deep grief over her death and a second time upon entering the house, so acutely hurting over Julie's behavior toward me. Brad wasn't worried about me because he saw me as quiet, easy, and willing to compromise, but he also felt that underneath I had the strength to survive anything. An eternal optimist, he was certain this was for the best and all would turn out well.

We set off for the attorney's office. Cy's secretary told us to make ourselves comfortable. Cy arrived shortly thereafter, and we set out for the short walk to the courthouse. When we arrived, Probate court was in session, so Cy led Brad and me to chairs down the hall and we waited for the courtroom to be vacated. Cy informed us that the attorneys would meet with the judge first and disappeared through a door near where we were seated. Julie and Jim had arrived and were seated by Chris Donovan farther down the hall. They avoided looking at Brad and me.

After fifteen minutes had passed, we were all ushered into the courtroom. Brad led me to a back row seat of the small room, where he could view everyone. Julie and Jim were seated on the opposite side of the room, ahead and to the right of where Brad and I sat. The probate attorney sat in front at a table and Cy Peters sat near him. My butterflies had quieted, but I didn't feel as quick and alert as I had wanted to for this day.

Court was called to order and Julie was called to the stand. The list I had submitted was presented to Julie, one item at a time. Cy questioned her first. She testified she knew of no ring of our grandfather's, that the Tiffany-like lamp was hers, and she just let her aunt use it as it had been given to her years ago. She continued with how she knew nothing about any pictures and denied the Nippon creamer and sugar were Aunt Beckie's, pieces that had surreptitiously been removed from the house before Brad and I had moved them. Julie insisted they had been Mother's designation to her and were always at the parental home. She denied having any silver at any time, testified the wooden silver chest had been given to Alison and that she had removed it because of the designation, denied there were any plates missing, and testified that the gold dust was gold dust paint from our aunt's paint supply. Chuckling at this lie, I had opened the door for Julie by giving her a choice on her list and she had chosen the less valuable option of gold dust paint, as I knew she would. This judge had jailed an heir for stealing gold coins, and I did not wish that for my sister. My intent was to get Julie to divide, not be criminally charged, though she probably deserved to be.

The testimony went on. Not only did Julie know nothing about silverware, but she also continued with knowing nothing about everything else on my list except the step ladder, which she explained they had removed from the house to repair. Brad looked at me with a huge grin on his face as we both knew the ladder was almost new and needed no repair. She admitted there were two Jim Lee oil paintings but claimed she didn't know where the second one was. Then she testified about the oil lamps. She stated her aunt had three but there were only two in the parental home and the third one had disappeared. I wasn't surprised, as it was the nicest one of the three. That is why it had been placed behind a lot of other articles on a high shelf in the summer kitchen. I fully realized why Julie had tried to paint me as mentally having a problem. She went on to state she only had one from Jim's mother's estate that had pretty marbles in it. Now I surmised Julie had never revealed to her family the note I had sent her, informing her where the third lamp could be found.

She further testified that when she arrived at our parents' house, the desk was wide open and empty of anything worth having. Once again, Brad and I looked at each other. The brown leather pouch with the gold dust was in the desk and gone when Brad and I returned in the spring. I recalled my family's trip west, which included Aunt Beckie, while Julie was away at nurses' training. We had been invited to Central City, Colorado by a couple who had been former students of Dad's and now owned a gold mine there. The trip had been such fun. Dad had taken me to see "The Face in the Barroom Floor." There were bullet holes in the room that Dad pointed out to me. We had stayed for four days and, when we left, the couple had given us several leather pouches full of gold dust. Mom and Dad's gold dust never surfaced at the house. Aunt Beckie had kept hers in her desk. Later, she had taken other trips west and had added to the gold dust every time she went. The leather pouch was almost completely full.

Bringing my attention back to the proceedings, I heard Julie admit to possessing her aunt's antique gold, ruby, and pearl necklace, alleging that Aunt

Beckie had given it to her. In my conversation with Julie, she had alleged the same thing. Our aunt had never mentioned this to me, and this struck me as strange, because the family had really tried to keep each other informed so there would be no misunderstandings. Knowing Julie as I now did, she was determined to keep every piece of family jewelry she could get her hands on and not divide a thing. That included my designated jewelry. Also, Aunt Beckie had been furious with Julie over money and her stealing from our parents.

Chris Donovan led the questioning with Julie's list she had submitted for me. The Nippon Julie named as missing had been brought to our parents' house and hidden away long before I moved anything from Aunt Beckie's. In moving things around in the cupboards to make room for Aunt Beckie's dishes, I had discovered them in the very back of a lower cupboard that was seldom accessed.

Julie testified a Nippon pin holder was missing when it had been sitting in Mother's curio cabinet where I had placed it after bringing it over from Aunt Beckie's. There were antique spritzer bottles, Julie alleged, and only one had been sold at the sale. She even went so far as to say she had personally seen five of them and they were worth twenty-five dollars each. Also missing, ten down pillows.

With Julie's testimony finished, it was my turn to take the stand. I testified there was only one spritzer bottle and I had bought it. Relieved I had spoken with Faith, I knew there had been only three originally. Faith had the names and addresses of the two people our aunt had given the other two bottles, as she didn't want to be blamed for anything missing at the house. Smart lady. That was also testified to in court.

What happened with the pillows was explained. At this point in the testimony, the Judge smiled at me and reminded me that all property was joint property, and nothing was to be removed without the other's consent. With what I perceived as a gentle tone, he told me the five pillows would have to be brought back. Later, I asked Brad why the judge had been so nice about this, and he explained it was because we had them washed and repaired and they had been shared. I wondered why Julie didn't have to bring the silver caddy back as she had removed it without my consent but concluded the judge had missed this in the litany of boring and not necessarily valuable items. Julie's list had included our maternal grandfather's watch, which I had also listed. Julie had the watch, I felt sure, and was trying to accuse me of something she herself had stolen. With Julie's game playing, one could never be sure where truth lay. In my testimony, I knew nothing about the watch and remembered Faith's information to me previously, "There was no jewelry in the house. It was all kept in a safe deposit box." Julie was the only one who had access because she was the Representative.

The same was stated about our aunt's missing gold bracelet and, since I had been given our maternal grandmother's gold bracelet at 14 years of age, I concluded that Julie was trying to cause me to lose it by implying that was the one missing. Too honest sometimes for my own good, I testified that I, indeed, did have a gold bracelet that had been in my possession since my youth. The judge questioned me as to how many years ago that was. With my answer, the matter was dropped. Julie had included on her list the fancy oil lamp too. She accused me of taking it and, even after I had written the letter explaining where it was in the house, she still saw fit to add that to the list as missing.

My testimony was that many things were moved in the house from time to time and things seemed to disappear and items changed around so frequently that it was difficult to account for them. The oil lamps were one of those items and I testified my sister continually disputed my count of these. I testified firmly I had no oil lamps other than those I had bought at the sale. Roseville pottery was the next item on Julie's list and her accusation was that the value ranged from $100 to several thousand dollars. She alleged that there were five pieces that our aunt owned for many years. I was so gratified Faith had kept track of contents as efficiently as she did. I testified that I only saw several badly cracked vases and that my grandparent's dinnerware had been nowhere in sight when I moved the items to the parental home. Faith hadn't seen any either, and she had worked there for over twenty years! I wasn't asked about the satin brocade fabric I had unwittingly removed to make that small tablecloth. I suspected the lawyer deleted it from his list.

Cy stepped forward and began his questioning. He started from the list Julie had testified about. He tried to bring out through his questioning that the Nippon could not have been from my grandmother's collection because it was a later design, but a similar pattern bought some eighteen years later by Aunt Beckie. Unfortunately, I couldn't answer his question appropriately to bring this out. He must have thought I was a dunce. He hadn't phrased the question in a way that I could help him. I answered that each piece was unique and easily identifiable, which didn't tie it directly to Aunt Beckie. He explained that the death certificate that was missing was far more ornate than the one returned in its place at the parental home. There had been two in the family. When I testified that grandfather's 18K gold and diamond ring had been designated to me and my sister had told me there was nothing in writing and had kept it, Julie and Jim snickered. I knew the lawyers couldn't see them, but I felt sure the judge could. What did he make of that reaction? Then I testified that the Tiffany-like lamp was 36 inches, not the 22 inches that had been on the inventory and was a quality piece bought by our grandfather from an estate sale and promised to my sister years ago. She was to have it following the death of our aunt.

The Judge told the probate attorney, who doubled as Julie's attorney, that he had not lost his defense that the gift of the lamp was a completed one, but that I could bring an appraiser to the lamp, which was at Julie and Jim's, to see if the value is correct. He warned the attorney that perhaps there should be a claim made for mysterious disappearance. The attorney continued to argue that I should also have to pay an appraised value for my items instead of the probate price and maintained that he did not want the appraisal done by a large gallery of high-end merchandise. The judge stood his ground and warned that he might rule that the lamp was not a completed gift. "The appraisal may be for $15,000. Surprise! It's yours, lady, pay the $7500! Be careful what you wish for, you might get it, understand that." He then added, "I always reserve the right and give the opportunity to revise this appraisal price submitted for $350. Do you?" There was no response to the judge's question.

Then I heard my sister say, "If I have to pay $7500, I don't want it!" I felt a pang of sadness. Jim and Julie could well afford the $7500 and Julie had, including the lake shore property and the contents from the house, deprived me of in excess of $25,000. However, for sisters to pay for designated gifts wasn't on my agenda in spite of what had been done to me.

The judge directed, "Try to resolve differences." I knew trying to work anything out with Julie was impossible—that was why I had to retain an attorney! Surely the judge realized this.

Cy continued with his questioning. I testified that, when I had returned to my parents' house eight weeks after the move, the desk had been broken into and the gold dust or gold dust paint and the gold buckle were gone, along with a fancy death certificate of our great grandfather's. I testified I had asked many times to divide contents from both estates, but all requests had been ignored. I stated I had copies of letters sent to my sister, but she had not responded. Those letters were presented. At this statement, Jim looked shocked and glared at Julie, who stared straight ahead. Then, I presented the inventory of the missing silver which had mysteriously reappeared, stating one set of forty pieces was still missing.

Testimony completed, the lawyers and judge withdrew to the judge's chambers and made their arguments there. When they returned to the courtroom, the judge began, "This is where one dispenses wisdom, supposedly. I'm not sure how we ever heal this family, two sisters polarized over something like this. Something isn't right, and I don't know how it has come to pass. It may be an irreconcilable rift. I'm sure that your aunt and your parents would rather have destroyed everything than have this happen. So, I'm going to do that for you. I hereby order that, today, a sheriff's deputy will accompany Mr. and Mrs. Latimer to the parental home while they collect their things, and the house is hereby sealed and house and contents to be sold in whatever way can be worked out. Josephine may take an appraiser to the Latimer home to appraise the Tiffany at fair market value. Keys to the home will be turned in now. Julie Latimer will be put under supervision as Representative. I would put her out as Representative, but there is only one more duty to perform. Court is adjourned.

I questioned the key situation as I had another setback in Illinois. I did not intend, however, to violate the court order. Julie, on the other hand, also had other sets to the house and given her rebellious nature, I surmised she probably would violate the order. It didn't occur to Brad or me to request the locks be changed.

Brad, Cyrus, and I walked back to the office and took our respective seats. There was silence, then Cyrus spoke, "Well, that decision wasn't against my client because you rarely use the house." Then he chuckled, "This is really frontier justice!" His comment puzzled me because I knew other families that had resorted to a court order to seal a house. It would be a while before I learned what "frontier justice" had been carried out.

"He was a nice judge," Brad said. "I've been in law enforcement for thirty-three years and I have seen people put in jail for less than what Julie did to Josie."

"It was a shock when he sealed the house," I said, "but I'm happy at the decision to sell. This was financially such a drain for me. I wasn't trying to claim a lot of things. If she just could have given me what was designated to me and just a few cherished items and my pictures, but she couldn't even do that."

Cy said, "She doesn't want you to have anything you want. If she knows you want something, she will take it. She shouldn't have answered the questions the way she did in court. She must have known the judge had all the facts. He would know she wasn't telling the truth. Chris told me after the adjournment that Jim asked if what you testified to about trying to divide with your sister was true. Chris told him you had been trying to divide for quite some time."

"My parents said they always hoped Jim would keep her on the straight and narrow. He must have known something about what was going on. I thought he was an honest person."

"From all we can gather, he is, but remember, he has to live with this woman! We were in the judge's chambers half chuckling over the disbelief we felt in trying to deal with your sister. The judge urged Chris to do what he could to bring the valuables back. If the amount of valuables is enough, she could be criminally charged, and I think Chris will tell her that."

"I wonder how she will react?"

"Well, we shall see." Cy replied. "She always has to have the edge and has absolutely no idea what fairness is. She stonewalls more than anyone I have ever dealt with. You really have to pin her to the wall, and she still manages to evade the question."

A date had been set for two weeks for bidding on Rebecca's Victorian cottage, the homestead. The more I thought about it, the more I felt I couldn't let it go. It needed renovation but had seven-inch-thick walls and double plank floors. It had been built in 1850 and my great grandparents had lived there and raised ten children. All this time I had been paying for a home I couldn't use but rarely, and the money had always been an issue. Now Brad would be retiring within the next five years, and we wanted a place of our own in our hometown that we could come to any time we wished. After all that had transpired at my parents' home, I had no desire to be there. It was simply too painful.

TWENTY-ONE

FINAL RESOLUTION

1993 - 2008

We visited Faith as she had requested following the court appearance. She greeted us warmly before pressing us about what had happened in court. Brad informed her Jim and Julie were being escorted from the house by a sheriff's deputy and the house would be sealed, and that keys were handed in at court. Brad went on to explain that Julie was under supervision as Representative, and that I could have put her out but there was very little left to do in the estate business.

Faith said, "I was called into the Inquiry but was not to reveal that until all was over. I explained about the items she accused you of taking. I'm pleased the judge put them out. I told them that Jim and Julie had "Squatter's Rights Fever." There were many times when her family wasn't there that they could have accommodated you and stayed at Jim's mother's house. Your sister implied you never came home and never saw your parents. I know you didn't come home much but I knew you always drove to Williamsport when your mother had to see the doctor, and you were always with them over the holidays. They asked about your dad's car, and I told them what he told me, that he was giving you the car as extra from his estate because he felt you needed the help."

So here was a third person Dad had told about the car and his intent. I felt even more vindicated.

"I also told them she took a terrible advantage of you," Faith went on. "You were so very sick and not yourself. The attorneys questioned me about the authenticity of your allegation regarding the gold dust. They also asked about your integrity. I told them there was gold dust and Julie brought it over to show me and said how very valuable it was. There was also a gold buckle with an engraved initial on it. They were skeptical as to why the gold dust wasn't on the inventory to begin with. I assured them it had probably been an oversight because you are not materialistic. You are more like Lee, whereas Julie was the opposite." Faith went on to relate the other questions the attorneys asked. "They asked about the Tiffany, and I told them I had cleaned it many times and it was very large. I said my guess was 36 inches."

"Why did she deny there was a Jim Lee oil painting?"

Faith had tears in her eyes, "Julie gave me the Jim Lee picture, but I will give it back if you wish. Also, she gave me a vacuum cleaner which I badly needed, and I would hate to give it back, but I will if you want. The ring is a perfect, blue, white diamond. Should I give that back?"

"Aunt Beckie loved you very much and wanted you to have the ring. You worked for her faithfully for twenty years. I am not upset about the oil painting or anything else. I just wanted to be told the truth. The things Aunt Beckie wanted you to have and the extra things you requested are not a problem. Please don't cry." With this, I hugged her.

"She accused you of stealing jewelry and they asked about that. There was no jewelry in the house and the only person who had access to the safe deposit boxes was Julie. You know I consider myself an honest person, and I didn't like the things I saw going on. We all have to look at ourselves from time to time in order to be a better person. I am convinced your sister never does. I don't know if you know this, but she rules her family with an iron hand. I have seen how subservient they are to her. The girls are in their thirties and are not allowed to speak about anything if they disagree with their mother."

Faith continued with more information. "The attorneys had asked what I thought of Jim. I told them, in my opinion, he was honest but didn't realize what was going on, probably wasn't paying close attention," then added, "I don't think Julie can look at herself. It would be too painful and everyone in her family believes everything she tells them."

Before we left, I hugged Faith and thanked her for telling the truth and helping me prepare for the Inquiry. "It must have been hard, and I know you think a lot of my sister and you don't know me as well."

"It wasn't hard. I don't like dishonesty. I consider myself an honest person, and I do know you, I know you very well from accounts by your aunt and Lee." She asked that we contact her again after the bidding on Aunt Beckie's home. She wished me good luck in trying to acquire it.

* * * * *

Brad and I returned to Illinois and a

few days later Cy called to inform us Chris Donovan had called to tell him that Julie wished to sell the house and, if I wanted to buy it, Julie would sell it for twice the realtor's evaluation and wanted twice the assessed value for the contents. I declined, not only because it was outrageous, but I loved the homestead. I spent many happy times there with my grandparents. To return to the parental home after all that had occurred, was simply too painful.

Three weeks later, just before Christmas, Brad and I were, once again, on our way to Michigan to bid on the homestead. I outbid the original buyer and was assured of closing by March. It was too cold to stay at the family farm, so we opted to stay at the motel. First, however, we made a trip to town to share our happy news with Faith. She offered to watch over the place and told us Julie had come to see her three days after Brad and I had left.

"She was crying over the house being sealed and said the judge had overstepped his authority. It didn't seem to occur to her she had overstepped hers. She is also threatening to back up a truck and take everything she wants. Be assured I will watch both places. Calling her on her behavior has made her more defiant, not contrite. I learned that the deputy followed them out of town all the way to Bay Harbor until they turned off the main road to go to Jim's mother's house."

Now I knew why our lawyer had called it "Frontier Justice," as he probably knew what the judge had specifically ordered.

The following day, Brad and I left for home and arrived in time to have a festive, happy Christmas with Vickie. Over the winter, and with the stress much reduced, I began to feel better and react more quickly to questions. At times when I was feisty, Brad laughingly commented I must be getting better. I developed a little better stamina but accepted the fact I was not one of those few who would fully recover. There were others with this illness that were unable to function at all, so in a sense my condition was a blessing. It could have been so much worse.

* * * * *

Several days after New Year's, the phone rang: it was a co-worker and friend of Sharon's. Sharon had unexpectedly passed away and the autopsy showed she had a massive heart attack. Sharon had no heart problems but worked in a high stress job in advertising. In my last conversation with her before the holidays, she had planned to visit relatives on Christmas.

What had happened? Her friend told me that she hadn't shown up for work, was found in bed on her left side. She had a high amount of alcohol in her system. Apparently, the heart attack had occurred during her sleep New Year's Eve.

I shed tears when I heard the news. In the last few years, Sharon had confided she had started coming home and drinking two large goblets of wine with dinner every night. Alarmed because of my experiences at the hospital working with patients with drug and alcohol problems, and my personal experiences, I informed her of the amount of normal intake, strongly urging her to follow it, and exclaimed how dangerous it was to drink in the way she was. She laughed at me and answered, "Oh, but it is so much fun!" Now, my oldest and dearest friend and most ardent supporter was gone. Brad drove me to the memorial service, where I had been requested to speak, but I was too heart broken and afraid of breaking down. Instead, I prepared a eulogy and another of her friends read it for me.

* * * * *

The following May, we headed for the hometown again as the judge wanted a report on what had transpired between the sisters. We met with Cy, and he seemed disappointed that the appraisal hadn't been done, but I told him I was grateful for the ruling and wished to follow my parents' and aunt's wishes. At least Julie would know I could have caused them to lose the lamp due to the high price, which they had indicated they didn't want to pay. The judge was apprised of my decision and the sisters' decision to have a tag sale rather than an auction. Julie rose to the occasion and stated the two lamps could be given to me as designated. Then, Jim spoke to the judge, "You overstepped your authority in sealing the house and decreeing it had to be sold, didn't you?"

"I may have. If you are unhappy with the decision, you can always appeal it."

"Why don't you bring everything back you took?" My question was directed to Julie.

She didn't answer, but Jim, who was so very nice and had a sweetness that was in such contrast to my sister, answered for her, "What about all that stuff you took back to Illinois?"

To think he had thanked Brad and myself for all the work we had done to save Aunt Beckie's contents "I have paid for everything I have, Jim."

As we left the courtroom, we heard

Julie say to Jim, "I needed the house for our family!" I wanted to go back and tell her there wouldn't have been a court session if she had been willing to compromise. She would still have use of the house. My impression was that her behavior hadn't set well with the judge and, in my mind, caused him to have her escorted from the house and out of town by the deputy. It was her own fault she had lost use of the house.

When we got to the car, Brad advised, "You answered Jim wrong. you should have said, 'I challenge you to name one thing I have taken.'" I acknowledged he was right.

We stopped at Cy's office and asked why there had been no closing on the house. Cy assured us the closing was now set for July and strongly urged us to immediately change the locks. By the time we walked back to the car, I began to wonder why he had been so adamant about the lock change, and how had he known we hadn't changed the locks? Anyway, why would we? We hadn't closed on the house yet.

On the way back to the family farm, we stopped to see Faith. As usual, we were warmly greeted with tea and cookies. We told her the closing would now take place in July and that Cy had insisted we change the locks on the homestead. Faith informed us that Julie had a key to the homestead.

"When I was there checking the house, I discovered the thermostat was way up. I called Julie and she admitted she had come in and turned up the thermostat. She said she had a special deal with the gas company to turn up the heat to get a better rate. She shouldn't have been in your house. I called the attorneys, but the furnace had run all of January and the bill was over four hundred dollars for that little house! I suppose the attorneys waited out the winter in case she did the same thing again. That's why I think they are late in closing. You are paying out of your own pocket, but she has to as well."

My thought was that Julie must have believed that the closing had occurred soon after the bidding and that I would be responsible for all the bills.

The next day, Brad changed the locks and found a nice flashlight on the kitchen counter, which Faith disavowed as hers.

Chris Donovan wrote a letter to Cy to request that I pay for the Philby's travel expenses to Dalton to bid against me. Cy replied that based on all the circumstances (he didn't explain what they were) the closing date would not occur until July 1. "We feel very strongly that your client should be solely responsible for the payment to the Philby's for travel expenses.

I would point out that your client, the personal representative, arranged to sell the property for a figure far below the true case value. Keep in mind that my client was not advised of the proposed sale nor given an opportunity to buy the property at the lower figure. My client ended up buying the property pursuant to her successful bid that equaled the true case value. Based on the above, the estate received considerably more, and your client received half of that. I suggest that the above scenario would indicate that your client should be happy to pay the money owed for the travel expenses."

* * * * *

A year later, the attorneys accompanied Julie, Jim, Alison, Brad, Vickie, and I to my parents' home to collect our childhood items and other property. Julie was able to take the brass deer, Noritake dishes, and buggy. She had surreptitiously returned the damask tablecloth she had stolen from my house and replaced the old cloth I had packed in the boxes with the damask cloth. She could not look at me. My hope was that maybe she had just a bit of healthy shame.

Walking through the place, I noticed things that made me believe my sister had entered the sealed house. Items that may not have been at the house just prior to it being sealed were now present. There was a large, frosted bowl unfamiliar to me in the packed boxes and, of course, my tablecloth. Was Julie trying to make it look like I was trying to smuggle a bowl out of the house not accounted for on the inventory, or did she think she could confuse me, not realizing I had regained my mental faculties. The sewing box Julie had requested after the house was sealed was not there.

Walking upstairs, Jim and Alison followed me while Alison made misinformed and erroneous statements and accusations. I felt sad for Alison that she had been so misled when previously she had made such accurate assessments of her mother's behavior. I loved her and held back my tears. Obviously, Julie's family had been seduced by her deception and manipulation and a myriad of other negative behaviors. In a sense, her family were victims too. I was able to ignore them and went about retrieving my childhood items.

I noted that my doll had come back minus its hat and shoes and the collectable dishes were back in a nicer box. The twin mattresses in the back bedroom had disappeared and had been replaced by very old ones. I wasn't sure when they had done that. *You'd think they weren't millionaires and had no money.* Peeking into Mom's storeroom on my way downstairs, I noticed the family projector. Would there be any pictures even available, as Julie had already stripped the house of all the family pictures from the paternal side of the family, those for the projector plus the antique portraits? I shut the storeroom door feeling a loss that hurt more than the other items she had taken from me. Oh well, as Benjamin Franklin said, "If you want to know the true character of a person, share an inheritance with him." Unknown to me, the projector would be gone the following year when the sale was held. Descending the stairs, Jim and Alison behind me, I noticed Mom's best lace tablecloth folded on the dining room table. That tablecloth would be gone, as well, before the sale was held, out of a home supposedly sealed.

Alison walked over to Vickie, who stood apart from everyone else. "Why is Aunt Josie doing this?"

"Ask my mother."

"No."

"There are a lot of things missing here."

"Well, we took a lot of things to protect them."

"You don't protect them, Alison, you divide them."

Later I learned Julie had donated historical items of our paternal grandfather's, some of which were given to a museum in her name only. It reminded me of the lakeshore property sold to the birdwatchers. She received a gift and yearly magazines for our donation in her name only.

Almost a year and a half later, the sale began. Brad and I were called to Cy's office. "Your sister is acting up again," he said. "She has to control everything. She is trying to change plans for the sale and made threats that the sale would just have to be postponed if she can't have her way. She is insisting her daughters have equal access to choosing what they want. There will be a delay until all of this can be worked out. I've never seen anything like it. I have always gotten families to compromise. It is the worst case I have ever had!"

He sounded totally frustrated. The inability to get Julie to compromise or negotiate made me fully realize something was very wrong with my sister. Cy's words jerked me back to the present. "What do you want?"

"It would seem she wants her

daughters on an equal footing with me. That is not acceptable. They aren't in the will, but they can come in. However, they cannot speak to their mother or collude with her in any way, and whatever they choose can only be theirs if I don't have it on my list. Also, if my sister and I choose the same things, I want us to throw dice to determine who gets first choice. If I do, it will be the first time I ever had first choice against my sister." Brad and Cy chuckled. I added, "I wonder how she would handle that?"

"There is another issue," Cy went on. "She wants you to have to pay for whatever you buy, upfront. Usually, the heirs choose what they want, and it is deducted from the sale of the contents. She is trying to make it very difficult for you."

Brad spoke up, "There will be money for her to choose what she wants."

Cy, obviously pleased, nodded affirmatively.

Prior to the sale, we were summoned to Chris Donovan's office to view pictures. Julie had apparently brought back the one drawer full she didn't want and was now willing to divide them! How magnanimous of her! Brad and I were to view them first.

We arrived and were seated in a back room of Chris' office where the box of photos had been placed. Among them were also some historical papers about our great grandfather that were tucked in an envelope that also contained old paid bills and my grandmother's will. I sorted through the pictures and chose several. I also asked for the historical papers as we owned the homestead, but I had no memorabilia. When we were finished, the secretary came back to mark inconspicuously what we had chosen, then she made an interesting comment, "I will put these back with the rest of the pictures, so she has no idea what you have chosen."

The strange part of this was that, when I received all the photos I had chosen, the historical papers on our great grandfather were missing. Had Julie removed them? They were the bulk of what had been in the envelope, and this left me with three or four old bills and my grandmother's will. It seemed unlikely the secretary would allow that, especially when she had made a comment that convinced me she knew my sister's penchant for depriving me of all that she could. The papers could have easily been recopied if we had both requested them. Later I learned she had sent the historical papers on the homestead to a cousin without my knowledge or consent.

The sale took place two months later.

Cy advised, "Don't let her know what you want by your actions and keep your list close to your chest so she can't see it. I'm sure she will try. It looks to me as though she doesn't want you to have anything you want."

Later, the lawyers changed the rules. I surmised it was because of what Cy anticipated. Now, each sister and family would view the contents, but at different times. We would make a list of the desired items. Brad was not to be allowed in the house, per Julie's demand, but the lawyers let him come in anyway and he sat with them in the living room as I made my way through the house. He was allowed to make choices in the barn.

Mary had prepared a beautiful tag sale. It brought tears to my eyes. Items were displayed on long tables with white table coverings. Everything looked well organized, clean, and attractively presented.

Julie had brought back our grandmother's pendant watch that had been designated to me, but not my grandfather's diamond ring. I would have had to pay for something that had been meant as a gift and was so offended I didn't try to buy it. Julie wanted it and would buy it, which would give her two, one for each of her daughters—probably her plan in the first place.

Vickie had driven to the hometown twice due to her Aunt Julie's ultimatum. The second time, she was successful and made her list several days after everyone else had gone through the house.

A few days after we had made our choices, arrangements were made for a meeting in Chris Donovan's office to divide the items we had chosen. There were twenty. Cy would accompany me as Brad could not be present. When we arrived, Brad waited in the outer office. Julie and Jim had arrived first and were seated in front of Chris' desk, talking and laughing amicably, Julie being her most charming self. Cy and I seated ourselves on the far-left wall.

My request to throw dice for first choice was honored. How would Julie handle it if she didn't throw a higher number, since she always had to be first in everything?

We rose from our chairs and threw a pair of dice in an open area of the floor. I threw "boxcars", a twelve. Then Julie threw hers for a total of three. I was to go first. Divine intervention. We returned to our seats, a look of displeasure on Julie's face.

As I took my seat beside Cy, he

whispered, "Be sure to choose the things you want the most before your sister does," and proceeded to point to the list of items Mary had prepared, lingering on the 1930s ornate bedroom set he knew I loved. Then he whispered, "If you get the gate-legged table and decide you don't want it, I will buy it from you."

"No, I want it," I replied laughingly. The division continued. I heaved a sigh of relief when it was all over. Cy and I left the office.

When my family home went up for sale, the local realtor was apprised by the attorneys to check with each sister as to our acceptance of any offer, as most people in the area believed Julie and Jim owned the house. Julie, who wanted me to pay double what the house was worth, now would accept one-third below the listed value from anyone else. I objected and told the realtor my desire to get the full price as the house had just gone on the market and was the best lot in town. The realtor agreed and the buyer paid the full price.

Julie never visited Faith again.

Now that chapter of my life was closed. There was a wonderful feeling of relief and a little euphoria once everything was finished. The best part: I was out from under the expense of a home I wasn't allowed to use. I hadn't minded that Julie wanted use of the house every holiday, but Faith was right. There were so many times when she and Jim were alone, and she could have accommodated us.

A few days later, the probate attorney called. They had found six old pictures that had been overlooked. Did I want them, or should they throw them away? I told them Brad would pick them up. To my delight, there were six small portraits of our maternal great grandparents, our maternal great, great grandparents and great, great grandmother who looked like my mother! There was a tin type of my great grandfather and wife and two children and there were two black tintypes which, when reproduced, were wonderful clear copies of our paternal great grandparents. What a treasure trove! Why had Julie left these behind? Didn't she know who they were?

Later, I learned that the whole probate fiasco could have been avoided. Mary, the assistant to the probate attorney, informed me that it is estimated by those involved in the probate process that sixty to eighty percent of families have trouble. That is a high number. I learned that trouble could be avoided by following a different path. When a will is made out, the attorney obtains a copy and, when he is notified of the death, immediately secures the house by changing the locks (which wasn't done in our case even though the judge had sealed the house) and appoints a Representative who is bonded, impartial, reputable, and definitely not a family member.

*   *   *   *   *

The homestead needed renovation, but we could make do. The only immediate change would be the removal of one wall between two bedrooms in order to have a large enough bedroom. This left one bedroom for Vickie.

We furnished the homestead with my parents' things. It felt good to be in my grandmother's house where I had spent so many happy hours.

In the year leading up to the sale, at times I was having nausea and severe fatigue. I barely got through the process of choosing photos at the lawyer's office. With the onset of the illness and the metabolic and chemical changes autoimmune disease brings, most of those affected develop allergies and sinus problems they never had before. I was one of those. The allergies caused excessive sneezing and a copious amount of nasal secretions only somewhat alleviated by antihistamines. We finished the probate business of division. From 2000 and over a few years I began to notice a very slight narrowing of my left nasal passage. *Was I imagining it?* Watching over the next several years, the change kept progressing and ever so slowly my hearing wasn't as acute. Headaches accelerated with more facial pressure. I mentioned it to my internist but he seemed to think nothing of it.

Finally in 2006, while still in Illinois, I consulted with two ENT specialists and, when they were told of my symptoms, each told me to irrigate my sinuses, which brought no change. My next physical was due and my medical internist prescribed the same treatment as the ENT doctors.

In 2008, discouraged at the lack of progress, I decided to try doctors in Michigan. I made an appointment with an allergist near my hometown. Three weeks later, we made the trip and arrived for my appointment, with the hearing loss worse and my nasal passage now totally closed off. The viral symptoms had grown much worse.

Dr. Berry, an attractive blonde woman, walked into the room, looked at me and said, "You're sick!"

Thank God somebody had finally noticed! She sent me immediately for blood work and told me she was sending me to the best ENT doctor she knew. She made the appointment for me, three days hence, and got his orders for a CAT scan of my head. She kept in contact with me throughout the entire process.

Before my appointment with the new ENT doctor, my cousin Kerry surprised us with a visit. She had never contacted me during all the fuss with Julie. I knew she had been at my parents' home visiting Julie every summer. Now, they visited Julie at their new home on the lake in Bay Harbor.

Kerry and I had always been close but, with the cessation of contact, I just assumed she had been influenced by Aunt Doris. On this day, Kerry was her most charming, funny, and enthusiastic self. As her sister-in-law used to say about her, "If you haven't met her or gotten to know her, you have really missed something."

Kerry was delightful company and stayed for about an hour. When she got up to leave, she said, "Just remember one thing: family is the most important thing and what you did is not good. I hope you can fix it."

I was too shocked to reply, and the old familiar feelings of dread and stress descended on me. *Did she mean going to court?*

"I wish all of you would become acquainted with the facts before forming an opinion, as it seems there is a lot the family doesn't know and maybe should try to find out." She did not answer and took her leave.

Three days later we traveled eighty miles to Pleasant Lake, a mid-sized city. I met with Dr. McKenzie. He was a tall, husky black man with a voice that reminded me of James Earle Jones. I complimented him on his beautiful speaking voice and asked if he was a singer. Laughingly, he said he only sings in the shower. He had grown up in our same town in Illinois and had visited a museum many times during his childhood where Brad, for a short time, had been head of security. We had a lively conversation about the city and the museum.

After he examined me and looked at the scan, he said, "You have the classic signs of a sinus tumor. What kinds of doctors have you been seeing?"

"Apparently not very good ones."

"How soon do you want surgery?"

"Yesterday."

"How about tomorrow?"

That afternoon my pre-admission bloodwork was done, and I was to arrive eleven the next morning for surgery.

When I awoke from the anesthesia, my

nose was packed and felt like I had been thrown from the operating table to the gurney. Every muscle in my back and chest hurt. Later that day, Dr. McKenzie came in to visit. When I asked about all the muscle discomfort, he informed me they had to give tiny drops of curare to assure I would stay quiet during the procedure. He informed me of a drain in my ear and assured me my hearing should come back. Also, he informed me the type of tumor I had was slow growing and had probably started some years ago. What that meant to me was that, amid the stress in dealing with my sister, the tumor had gotten its start. He informed me, "The tumor was so large, I had to bring it down through your mouth. I have never removed one nearly as large. It looks terrible. I am sending it to the path lab. You have a hole in your sinus wall a Mac truck could drive through."

The following day, before I was released, the packing was removed, and I was given post-op instruction. The doctor's directions were to stay dry with an antihistamine and after the post-op check be seen every few years. He called several times during my recovery, as did the allergist.

When the pathology report came back, it was an inverted papilloma, a benign, highly aggressive and dangerous type tumor. Thankfully it wasn't cancer. I counted my blessings. As a result, the tumor caused optic nerve damage. The partial, upper inner aspect of the visual field of my left eye was gone.

Three days after the surgery, the allergist called and asked me to come in to see her. I was still swollen, bruised, and not feeling very well but I would have done almost anything she asked. When she entered the examining room, I rose from my chair, teary-eyed, and gave her a warm hug and thanked her. She hugged me back and said, "I'm so glad I could help you." I couldn't thank her enough. We talked awhile and I was to return for allergy tests when feeling better.

About a month after the surgery, my cousins called and were the nicest they had been to me since lawyers came into the mix. We had many pleasant conversations after that.

There are tinges of sadness at what actions I had to take, but Faith and Cy gave me hope which helped sustain me through my long ordeal. I have never regretted the decisions I made. I am at peace.

EPILOGUE

Eventually, Brad and I remarried, and his entire extended family welcomed me back. I have regained my serenity so crucial to my well-being in dealing with this autoimmune illness. Time heals all wounds. At ten years, my recovery, physically, has progressed as far as it can. My body cannot tolerate change. Staying on the same schedule enhances my impaired energy level. Vickie often says if we do anything outside of our "schedule" we get punished! There are still GI disturbances, food intolerances, headaches, fibromyalgia-like aching and joint pain. Mentally, I have recovered my alertness and perspicacity. I have never been able to return to work.

The homestead was renovated, and we eventually lived there full time. Vickie moved to the hometown as well and lives about one mile from us. She married and has one daughter, but she is no longer able to work her part-time job. She struggles with her poor energy level and at times looks totally depleted. Too much activity can trigger the pre-leukemic like blood dyscrasia which, with time and rest, will retract. My fear is, as she ages, the blood dyscrasia will morph into leukemia. She has a sleep disorder, anxiety, a panic disorder and also suffers from brain fog, some days being better than others. She still has trouble with mornings. If we are awakened outside of our schedules, we feel sick and viral. She often wears a shirt that says, "I don't do mornings." People laugh as it seems humorous: little do they realize it is the truth.

Recently she told me that, when she was a little girl, she would wake up in the morning and feel very ill. She forced herself to get ready for school and never complained because she thought everyone felt that way in the mornings. In the last year, she has developed kidney stones with an array of uncomfortable physical symptoms. This kidney condition may be due to the change in metabolism that comes with the autoimmune illness. Her one bright spot is her physician, who understands what she struggles with and does all he can to ease her symptoms.

Recently, she applied for disability when she could no longer work part-time. It seems they think she can work even though doing so causes another blood dyscrasia and even more intense fatigue. She got an advocate and recently appeared in front of a Judge who ruled she should be able to do some kind of low-level work. Vickie said she knew she was in trouble when the Judge couldn't pronounce "dyscrasia."

I happened to read the book, *Plague of Corruption* by Dr. Judy Mitkovits and Kent Heckenlively JD and learned the retroviral origin of ME/CFS, Autism, HIV-AIDS, and some prostate cancers. Doctors were not informed of these findings by scientists, and now I understand why it took twenty-two years to diagnose Vickie. Approximately ten million children and adults have been affected because of the retrovirus. Dr. Mitkovits now works on finding therapeutic measures.

ACKNOWLEDGEMENT

The events described in this true story could not have had the outcome they did without an astute and very wise attorney, Cy, and a wonderful woman we call "Faith". She was a godsend. Without her help, the outcome might have been quite different. Her reputation preceded her as an honorable person. Most of all, she gave me hope which helped sustain me through the long ordeal. Her words of wisdom and my attorney's observations and assessments still resonate with me today. My thanks to my editor Krista Hill for her invaluable suggestions and guidance, my family for their love and support for this project when the increased activity meant increased exacerbations. And lastly, but certainly not least, my granddaughter Jessica who did the initial computer work on the first draft but became ill. Kristen Taber took it from there with enthusiasm and dedication and considered it a "labor of love."

ABOUT THE AUTHOR

Josephine Walden

Josephine was raised in a quaint small town in "the thumb" of Michigan in a close extended family. Music and nursing were her passions. She became a psychiatric nurse and worked while her husband attended college. Work opportunities took them to Chicago. Years later they returned to "the thumb" and renovated her ancestral home. She enjoys her daughter and granddaughter who live nearby. "The Ordeal" is her first book and she is working on another true story involving hardship and duplicity.

Made in the USA
Monee, IL
14 July 2023